The *De vulgari eloquentia*, written by Dante in the early years of the fourteenth century, is the only known work of medieval literary theory to have been produced by a practising poet, and the first to assert the intrinsic superiority of living, vernacular languages over Latin. Its opening consideration of language as a sign-system includes foreshadowings of twentieth-century semiotics, and later sections contain the first serious effort at literary criticism based on close analytical reading since the classical era. Steven Botterill here offers an accurate Latin text and a readable English translation of the treatise, together with notes and introductory material, thus making available a work which is relevant not only to Dante's poetry and the history of Italian literature, but to our whole understanding of late medieval poetics, linguistics and literary practice.

Cambridge Medieval Classics 5

Dante, *De vulgari eloquentia*

Cambridge Medieval Classics

General editor

PETER DRONKE, FBA

Professor of Medieval Latin Literature, University of Cambridge

This series is designed to provide bilingual editions of medieval Latin and Greek works of prose, poetry, and drama dating from the period *c.* 350 – *c.* 1350. The original texts are offered on left-hand pages, with facing-page versions in lively modern English, newly translated for the series. There are introductions, and explanatory and textual notes.

The Cambridge Medieval Classics series allows access, often for the first time, to outstanding writing of the Middle Ages, with an emphasis on texts that are representative of key literary traditions and which offer penetrating insights into the culture of medieval Europe. Medieval politics, society, humour, and religion are all represented in the range of editions produced here. Students and scholars of the literature, thought, and history of the Middle Ages, as well as more general readers (including those with no knowledge of Latin or Greek) will be attracted by this unique opportunity to read vivid texts of wide interest from the years between the decline of the Roman empire and the rise of vernacular writing.

Opening titles

Other titles in preparation

Dante
De vulgari eloquentia

EDITED AND TRANSLATED BY

STEVEN BOTTERILL

University of California, Berkeley

CAMBRIDGE
UNIVERSITY PRESS

Published by the Press Syndicate of the University of Cambridge
The Pitt Building, Trumpington Street, Cambridge CB2 1RP
40 West 20th Street, New York, NY 10011-4211, USA
10 Stamford Road, Oakleigh, Melbourne 3166, Australia

First published 1996

A catalogue record for this book is available from the British Library

Library of Congress cataloguing in publication data applied for

ISBN 0 521 40064 3 hardback

Transferred to digital printing 2004

CE

Contents

Introduction

Dante Alighieri (1265–1321) has been famous to every generation since his own as the author of the *Divine Comedy* – even though that title, now so indissolubly linked with his name, was coined not by Dante himself, nor even in his lifetime, but (in 1555) by an enterprising Venetian publisher called Lodovico Dolce, who presumably hoped that the addition of so striking an epithet to the flatly generic appellation *Commedia* would help boost sales of his new edition of the text. Revered by many and reviled by a few, but never ceasing to be attentively read and analysed even in periods (such as the 'enlightened' eighteenth century) that found it difficult to understand or appreciate, the *Comedy* has, by virtue of its enormous celebrity and influence, firmly established the image of Dante as, first and foremost, a poet. Although it consistently gives the clearest imaginable evidence of the extraordinary range of Dante's intellectual interests, and although many have consequently been tempted to see it as a kind of encyclopaedia (or, in medieval terminology, a *summa*) of the multifaceted reality of European culture in the late Middle Ages, there can be little doubt that the *Comedy* is remembered by its readers, above all, as a *poem*, and that the primary impression it makes is achieved through Dante's mastery – instantly recognised by his contemporaries, not to mention by Dante himself – of the resources and techniques of poetic narrative. It is, then, his achievement as a poet rather than his distinction as a thinker that has earned Dante his canonical status in the history of world literature.

One result of the canonisation of the *Comedy* has been the serious critical and scholarly neglect of Dante's other writings. It is traditional in Italy to refer to these as the poet's 'opere minori', and the phrase's unmistakable note of disparagement is not altogether unjustified – most writings look 'minor' in the shadow of the *Comedy.* Dante himself, indeed, seems to have had no doubt that the poem was the culmination of his literary career, and his final statement on the many urgent issues that had preoccupied him throughout his adult life. It is as fascinating as it is useless to speculate as to what kind of poetry, if any, Dante might have written in the vernacular *after* the *Comedy*; *Paradiso* in parti-

cular would have been the proverbially hard act to follow. (The second of his Latin *Eclogues*, addressed to Giovanni del Virgilio, probably dates from 1320–1, and may thus have followed the completion of *Paradiso*; but, even if it did, it is not easy to see it as in any sense a new departure.) From one end of the *Comedy* to the other, however, Dante shows an interest in recalling, and building upon, the achievement of his 'minor' works, that later readers – especially outside Italy – have, unfortunately, seldom shared.

None of the several works of Dante's that preceded or accompanied the *Comedy's* composition – from the early sonnets of the 1280s to the Latin *Eclogues* and the (still disputed) *Quaestio de situ et forma aque et terre* of 1320–21 – enjoyed anything like the same degree of acclaim, in the fourteenth century or afterwards; and some of them underwent centuries of neglect – during which they came close to disappearing from view altogether, for lack of interest in producing new manuscripts or, later, printed editions – before the historical and philological scholarship of the nineteenth and twentieth centuries rescued them from the brink of oblivion. To this day, the endlessly expanding universe of academic Dante studies is much more intensely concerned with the *Comedy* than with any of Dante's other works, as a glance at the indices of the leading journals in the field will quickly make clear.

There is, perhaps, nothing wrong with this in principle – except that critical neglect of the 'opere minori' almost always produces fatally enfeebled readings of the *Comedy*. Just as Dante himself took the rest of his life's work for granted during the composition of his masterpiece – drawing on it for material, expanding on or correcting its arguments and conclusions, even, on occasion, referring to it directly, through thematic allusion or textual citation – so the reader who wishes to follow the poem's protagonist as closely as possible on the journey from 'selva oscura' to 'candida rosa' should have at least a passing familiarity with this most immediately relevant area of the *Comedy's* cultural prehistory. Though a lively debate still surrounds the question of Dante's reading of other authors and its effect on the text of the *Comedy*, there is no room for doubt that among the most influential writers he read was his own younger self.

This image of Dante as an assiduous re-reader of his own early writings is of considerable importance for our understanding of the 'opere minori' in general and of the *De vulgari eloquentia* in particular. Twentieth-century readers of Dante's minor works have too often overlooked the importance in most of them of the principle and practice of *commentary*; they have failed, that is, to pay sufficient attention to the fact that

each of the substantial (if in two cases uncompleted) volumes that
Dante compiled or composed before undertaking work on the *Comedy* –
the *Vita nuova* of 1293–5, the *Convivio* of 1304–7, and the *De vulgari elo-
quentia* itself – is conceived primarily as an exercise in the technical
analysis, by a poet, of instances of his own literary production.
This is not to deny, of course, that each of these works exhibits
other interests or gives voice to other concerns; or that, especially in the
case of the *Vita nuova*, those other interests and concerns have always
had a more immediate appeal to a wider readership than the specifically
poetic preoccupations of the elements of commentary that they
contain. (Barbara Reynolds's piercing insight, in the introduction to her
Penguin translation, that 'the *Vita nuova* is a treatise by a poet, written
for poets, on the art of poetry' is still fiercely resisted by the many lovers
of allegorical arcana and sentimental fiction who continue to busy
themselves with Dante's 'little book'.) The point still needs to be made,
however, that throughout his early career – and no less so in the
Comedy itself – Dante is keenly, indeed almost obsessively, concerned
with the definition and critical assessment of his own achievement as a
poet, and that the means through which he seeks to secure these ends
are those supplied by a pre-existing tradition of commentary on literary
texts. It is on this basis that he constructs the three very different
textual artefacts that are the *Vita nuova*, the *Convivio*, and the *De vulgari
eloquentia*.
Thus the *Vita nuova*, as well as the collection of lyric poems linked
by apparently (but deceptively) autobiographical prose that has made it
famous, includes passages of precise formal and structural analysis of
the large majority of its thirty-one poetic texts. Readers from Giovanni
Boccaccio in the fourteenth century to Dante Gabriel Rossetti in the
nineteenth – and beyond – have found these passages, brief as most of
them are, unbearably arid: Boccaccio copied them only in the margins
of his own copy of the *Vita nuova*, and recounted a (no doubt apocry-
phal) tale to the effect that Dante himself, late in life, had expressed
regret at having included them in the first place; Rossetti, wearied
beyond endurance by the effort of translating them, delegated the task
to his less fastidious brother; and they were omitted altogether from the
first printed edition, in 1576, and from more than a few of its successors.
But there they are, in spite of all, in the text; and their stubbornly unsen-
timental presence is a crucial part of what the *Vita nuova*, as a coherent
whole, is intended to be and to do.
The same is true of the *Convivio*, which, although clearly intended
as an elementary exposition of a variety of key philosophical issues in

Dante's culture, and thus as a work in a non-poetic (and arguably non-literary) genre, none the less takes the form, even in its unfinished state, of a set of close textual readings of lyric poems of Dante's own composition. In a word, it is made up of commentaries. And the *De vulgari eloquentia*, as we shall see when we come to discuss it in detail below, is also, at least in part, intended as an illustration and defence of Dante's thinking about, and practice of, the uniquely demanding art of the vernacular poet. From beginning to end of his mature poetic career, from the first chapter of the *Vita nuova* to the closing cantos of *Paradiso*, Dante thinks and writes not just as poet but as critic – and perhaps, in modern terms, also as theorist. Yet throughout, I insist, the urgent need to understand his own practice of poetry remains the focal point of both his literary invention and his critical thinking; and the analysis of his own poetry is always among the purposes for which a given text – even the *Comedy* – is called into being.

Dante's 'opere minori', then, should be read; and they should be read at least partly with an eye to the light they can throw on their author's conception of poetry, and on his most compelling realisation of that conception, the *Comedy*. But there is an obvious danger here. Reading the minor works *only*, or even chiefly, as accompaniment, background, or prolegomena to the *Comedy* carries with it certain interpretative perils. It is all too easy, when so doing, to be misled into the anachronistic assumption that Dante's literary production forms a seamless whole, whose (omniscient) author already had every detail of his forthcoming poem in mind when working on the 'opere minori'; and that, therefore, every detail of those 'minor' texts, however puzzling or rebarbative, can and should be reconciled or harmonised with the 'major' poem, to which they were deliberately designed as an introduction. (Readers of this stamp tend to experience agonising difficulties when, as is not infrequently the case, the arguments and conclusions of the 'opere minori' and the *Comedy* turn out to be, quite simply, irreconcilable.) Such reading also runs the risk of creating an equally unsatisfactory (because excessively narrow) approach to these texts, in which they are read exclusively in relation to their author's other work, as if they had been written in complete isolation from any surrounding culture – rather than opening out the discussion to include other, perhaps more relevant or illuminating, writings in the same or similar genres from the pens of other authors.

Both these alternatives should be avoided: the first because it is inherently implausible (the Dante of the mid-1290s cannot have had the course of his life and writing over the next quarter-century already

mapped out before him, and the minor works were surely conceived as independent entities – even if they do all derive from the same matrix of concerns that, eventually, also generated the *Comedy*); the second because some at least of those other writings were certainly available and important to Dante, and it can only add to our understanding of his work if we have a reasonably clear sense of the immediate cultural context within which that work was produced.

Rather, then, than exploring the minor works solely for what they can tell us about the *Comedy*, a more productive approach would, in my opinion, both read them on the terms they themselves dictate, as interesting and valuable texts in their own right, and also attempt to relate them to the output of writers (especially in the field of poetic commentary) perhaps less celebrated but no less significant, at least in the history of ideas, than Dante Alighieri. We need, in brief, diachronic readings of Dante's career that stop short of, rather than beginning with, the 'poema sacro', as well as synchronic readings of his culture that compare the 'opere minori', where possible, with other examples of their various genres, rather than with the wholly – and truly – incomparable *Comedy*. It is my hope that the present translation will facilitate this process, at least as far as the *De vulgari eloquentia* is concerned.

And it is to the *De vulgari eloquentia* that we must now turn.

The text known to modern times as the *De vulgari eloquentia* – though whether this was Dante's title for it is not clear – is an unfinished Latin treatise on language and poetry, consisting of two Books, one of nineteen chapters and one of fourteen, probably written in the early years of Dante's exile from Florence. Internal evidence makes at least an approximate dating possible: Dante describes himself (Book I, chapter vi) as already suffering in exile, which indicates a date after 1302; and he makes a delicate but pointed allusion (II. vi) to the failed Sicilian expedition of the French prince Charles of Valois, which took place in August 1302. Elsewhere (I. xii), he lists Giovanni I of Monferrato among the malignant warlords who currently infest the Italian peninsula; Giovanni died in February 1305. These dates, then, seem to mark the broad limits within which the *De vulgari eloquentia* was composed; and if we are to take at face value a reference in Book I of the *Convivio* (itself probably dating from 1302 or 1303) to Dante's intention to write, at some unspecified time in the future, a treatise 'di Volgare Eloquenza' (*Convivio* I. v. 9), it seems plausible to argue that work on the latter is unlikely to have begun much before 1303, and was probably complete by early 1305. (It is possible, of course, that Giovanni of Monferrato's death

occurred after *De vulgari eloquentia* I. xii was written but while Dante was still working on the rest of the book; yet, even if this were the case, it is hard to see how the writing of what is, after all, a comparatively brief text, can have occupied Dante much beyond the end of 1305.) All things considered, 1303-5 seems to be a reasonable time-frame for the composition of the *De vulgari eloquentia*: ten years after the *Vita nuova*, roughly contemporary with the *Convivio*, and still a few years before the beginning of *Inferno*.

By early 1303, Dante Alighieri already had behind him two careers, as lyric poet and municipal politician, the first as distinguished as the second was disastrous; and he was emerging from a time of political turmoil and, no doubt, personal confusion, which had seen him involved first in the Florentine 'revolution' of 1300–1 and then, after his faction's defeat and expulsion from the city, in a variety of ineffectual attempts by the expelled to regain the power of which they had been so brutally deprived. All the evidence suggests that Dante quickly grew disenchanted with the machinations of his fellow 'fuorusciti', and instead directed his energies, as the first decade of the fourteenth century wore on, towards a programme of thinking and study based on his reading (or in some cases re-reading) of the most culturally potent writings he could find, in several fields of knowledge. The exact extent and, still more, the detailed sequence of this reading remains controversial and no doubt ultimately irrecoverable; but it seems clear from later developments that, in the aftermath of the disappointment of all his most cherished hopes for earthly success, Dante underwent at this time an experience of profound and searching self-examination, which led him to try to rebuild the moral and intellectual structure of his personality from the foundations. This process seems to have involved intense reflection on his own earlier life and literary work – especially those parts of both life and work connected with his love for Beatrice Portinari – as well as the acquisition of a greater familiarity with the authoritative writings of his predecessors in poetry, poetics, history, political theory, natural and moral philosophy, biblical exegesis, spirituality, and theology. And although the most tangible fruit of Dante's experiences after 1300–1 was to be the *Comedy*, the *De vulgari eloquentia* also fits into this context. For an ostensibly impersonal, even scientific, study, it is markedly personal in tone throughout; and it resounds from beginning to end with Dante's unmistakably individual commitment to the values – intellectual, ethical, linguistic, even political – in which it deals.

'End', of course, is the wrong word to use of the *De vulgari eloquentia*:

for the book was not finished. The text that we have today trails off in
the middle of a chapter (II. xiv), and there is no evidence, either in the
meagre manuscript tradition or elsewhere, that any more was ever
written. (It has recently been suggested, by Warman Welliver, that
Dante's failure to complete his work was a deliberate move on his part,
intended to inculcate a moral lesson about the inadequacy of human
language; but this view has found few adherents.) Since the treatise
itself includes more than one statement of its author's intention to
discuss various topics in later Books than those that have survived, it is
usually assumed nowadays that Dante did at least plan to complete
the *De vulgari eloquentia* (though few if any believe that he actually did
so, and thus that the rest of the work has simply disappeared). Its frag-
mentary state is normally attributed by modern scholarship to any one
or combination of a number of external causes – perhaps no more than
loss of interest, perhaps the distractions and complications of the
exiled author's wandering life, perhaps – a hypothesis that many find
particularly attractive – Dante's growing realisation that his views on
poetic language were best expounded not in theory but in practice. (On
this view, completion of the *De vulgari eloquentia* would have been sacri-
ficed to the demands of the project that eventually became the
Comedy.) At all events, the discussion of vernacular poetry begun in
Book II is seriously truncated, and leaves out numerous topics with
which Dante might have been expected to engage, and on which his
views would certainly have been worth hearing. The list of these ap-
parent lacunae is a long one and in many ways a source of regret – a
good deal of scholarly energy could have been saved, for instance, if the
future author of the *Comedy* had ever fulfilled his promise, made in *De
vulgari eloquentia* II. iv, to define with precision just what he understood
the comic style in poetry to be, by distinguishing its nature and require-
ments from those of its tragic and elegiac counterparts.

Discussion of what the *De vulgari eloquentia* might have become is
an interesting but not very profitable entertainment; for the moment it
will be enough to consider Dante's work as it stands. The book has been
transmitted in a very small number of manuscripts, only three of
which are recognised as having value for the establishment of an accu-
rate text. Two of these, both copied during the fifteenth century from
lost earlier exemplars and known today as *G* and *T*, were available when
the first printed edition was prepared at Paris in 1577, ironically
enough by another exiled Florentine, Jacopo Corbinelli; the third,
which is also the oldest, having been copied in the mid or late four-
teenth century, remained entirely unknown until it was identified in

1917 in a library in Berlin. The discovery of the so-called 'codice berlinese' (B) helped to clear up a number of obscurities in the *De vulgari eloquentia*'s textual tradition, and there is an unusual degree of consensus among scholars on the subject today. (The two most useful and reliable editions to appear since the Second World War, those of Aristide Marigo and Pier Vincenzo Mengaldo, differ substantially on scarcely more than half-a-dozen textual readings, none of which seriously affects the tenor of Dante's argument.) We can, then, be reasonably confident – perhaps as confident as it is ever possible to be when dealing with a medieval text – that what we read in the *De vulgari eloquentia* is identical, or very nearly so, with what Dante wrote.

Unusually for a medieval work of what would nowadays be called 'non-fiction', the *De vulgari eloquentia* begins not with a tribute to its author's intellectual ancestors, but with a resounding declaration of his own absolute originality: 'Since I find that no one, before myself, has dealt with the theory of eloquence in the vernacular... I shall try... to say something useful about the language of people who speak the vulgar tongue' (i. i). Only after this does Dante acknowledge, in more characteristically medieval fashion, his debt to other authorities: 'Yet, in so doing, I shall not bring to so large a cup only the water of my own thinking, but shall add to it more potent ingredients, taken or extracted from elsewhere' (i. i). This mellifluous opening paragraph, whose graceful Latinity amply demonstrates its author's qualifications as a user of language (though ironically so, given that his subject is not Latin eloquence but its 'vulgar' counterpart), offers an interestingly piquant blend of authorial pride and humility. Its self-depreciating reference to Dante's own ideas as 'water' in comparison with the 'potent ingredients' supplied by others does not suffice – and was clearly not intended – to dilute the splendidly self-confident affirmation with which this work begins: that no one, in the whole course of human intellectual history, has ever attempted to tackle Dante's subject before. Dante is not, at the best of times, a writer whose protestations of modesty (false or otherwise) carry much conviction; yet the seemingly arrogant claim he makes in the *De vulgari eloquentia*'s opening sentence is eminently justified. Even though the later Middle Ages had already produced many commentaries on literary texts, several major works of poetics, and a fair amount of theoretical writing about language (especially that of the so-called *modistae* or speculative grammarians), Dante's contribution to the field was, and remains, unique.

What makes it so is the extraordinary variety of its author's intellectual interests, the flexibility and diversity of the analytical methods he

employs and the sources on which he draws, and the authority con-
ferred on his argument – especially in the discussion of vernacular lyric
poetry in Book II – by his experience as a practitioner in the field to
which that argument refers. Even within its unnaturally restricted
compass, the *De vulgari eloquentia* fruitfully combines a number of
branches of knowledge that medieval tradition had previously tended
to separate: it brings together rhetorical and factual elements drawn
from the realms of history, geography, philosophy, biblical exegesis and
political theory, as well as the fundamentally linguistic matters that are
its professed concern, in a way that is not, by and large, characteristic
of any of the more narrowly definable genres of medieval writing about
language or literature.

Though Dante's work partakes to some extent of each of the relevant
contemporary traditions or genres (commentary, poetics, rhetoric,
speculative grammar), it belongs whole-heartedly to none of them –
which is, perhaps, only a way of saying that it belongs equally to them
all. It is, indeed, the success with which Dante achieves a remarkable
series of cultural integrations – of academic theory with poetic practice,
of historical analysis with contemporary observation, of abstract princi-
ples with empirical reality – of, in a word, linguistics with literature
(and of both these with politics) – that makes his aborted treatise both
so difficult to categorise and so perennially fascinating to read. And it
might also be said that the *De vulgari eloquentia*'s very multiplicity of
issues and approaches licenses the several recent readings (pre-
eminent among them that of Marianne Shapiro) that have sought to es-
tablish for it a deeper significance than any normally allowed it by cri-
tical tradition – have sought, that is, to read its text in an essentially
allegorical fashion, and to argue that its true import is something very
different from the technical interest in linguistic and literary issues that
dominates it at the surface level. Only because this book *is* so patently
interested in matters other than those which form its ostensible subject
– or rather, perhaps, because Dante's preoccupation with language
and literature inevitably expands to include and inform all the other
areas of intellectual activity with which he was concerned – does it
become possible, and even convincing, to argue that we are dealing, in
this case, with something more than a mere textbook of linguistics or
manual of poetic technique.

The first chapter of the *De vulgari eloquentia*, then, defines the pre-
mises on which the whole work (had it ever been a whole) would have
been based. The book's subject is to be 'the language of people who speak
the vulgar tongue', the vernacular which 'infants acquire from those

around them when they first begin to distinguish sounds' (I. i). Dante distinguishes sharply and crucially between this and another kind of language, 'which the Romans called *gramatica*, and which can only be learned 'through dedication to a lengthy course of study' (I. i). Unlike the vernacular, this is not available to all peoples; and even among those peoples who do possess it (the Greeks and some others, as well as the Western European heirs of classical Latin), not every individual is able to 'achieve complete fluency' in it. The vernacular, then, is natural, universal and learned almost by instinct; its counterpart is none of these things. And of these languages, says Dante in a sentence as unassuming as it is revolutionary, 'the more noble is the vernacular'. A natural, spoken, living language – like Italian – is, axiomatically, *superior* to an artificial, unspoken, dead one – like Latin. This is a moment of extraordinary significance in Italian, indeed Western, cultural history; it is the Declaration of Independence of the 'modern languages'.

It is worth repeating that the vital distinction here is not so much between two particular languages – Italian and Latin – as between two different *kinds* of language, one 'natural' and one 'artificial'; even though, in the specific cultural circumstances of Dante's Italy, those two kinds were indeed exemplified, respectively, by Italian (in its various forms) and Latin, the basic conceptual scheme would be valid in any other time and place. (The vernacular of the Greeks, for instance, is obviously not Italian, and their 'artificial' language would presumably not be Latin.) In the terminology of the *De vulgari eloquentia*, then, 'vernacular' and 'Italian' are by no means strictly synonymous; Dante's argument about the vernacular is as true of *all* vernaculars, in the abstract, as it is of Italian in the concrete. Only the fact that Italian is *his* vernacular, and thus the example (literally) on the tip of his tongue, singles it out as the basis of his treatise. And the desire to deal both with general principles of language and with their particular instantiation in the Italian peninsula in the early fourteenth century not only underlies the whole *De vulgari eloquentia* but helps to explain its (albeit fragmentary) structure. Dante is anxious to begin his study of 'eloquence in the vernacular' (I. i) from first principles, which means that the way for his account of the varieties of Italian extant in his own time must be prepared by a history not just of Italian but of all human language, beginning in the Garden of Eden; and this in turn must be preceded by a philosophical explanation of language as a concept.

Accordingly, the second chapter of Book I defines language as a uniquely human attribute, shared by neither animals nor angels, and thus

serving as an indispensable marker of a truly human nature. It would be hard to over-estimate the importance of this point: the urgency of Dante's concern with language, in all his work, stems precisely from the fact that, for him, to use language was to be human (and vice versa), and to use language badly (inaccurately, inelegantly, immorally) was to surrender some vital part of one's humanity. In his view, as expounded here, language exists for the sole purpose of enabling human beings to communicate to each other the concepts they form in their minds (i. ii); it is thus the indispensable vehicle of mediation between the individual and the social, making possible not just personal relationships among human beings but also larger social structures and, ultimately, human civilisation as a whole. Linguistic shortcomings in an individual can thus be seen – as Dante himself, especially in *Inferno*, invariably sees them – as also being offences against both the concept and the practice of community.

Dante next moves on (i. iii) to consider the specific nature of language itself, and argues, in an analysis that shows a number of fascinating premonitions of twentieth-century theories (but is also, as too few modern theorists are aware, based on ideas familiar in the West since classical times), that language is a system of signs, in which a conventional or arbitrary sound or image is accepted, by users of a given language, as representing a particular mental construct. Dante's key words in this argument are 'rational', for the mental construct, and 'perceptible', for the conventional sound or image; and there is enough of a correspondence here with the notions of 'signifié' and 'signifiant' in modern semiotics to encourage a closer comparison than space, on this occasion, will permit – though it may be noted, for instance, that although Dante identifies signs and their arbitrariness as the basis of language as a system, he does not anticipate the stress on relationships *between* signs, especially the ways in which they differ, that has been at the heart of semiotics since Saussure.

These two chapters of preliminary definition are followed by an account, cast in substantially biblical, not to say theological, terms, of the historical foundations of human language. Having decided, in other words, what language is, Dante proceeds, in *De vulgari eloquentia* i. iv–vii, to enquire where it came from. His answer – ultimately derived, of course, from the text of the Bible and from several centuries of Christian commentary thereon – is that the first speaker was Adam (though here he has to perform a certain amount of exegetical acrobatics, since the Bible itself seems to give the primacy on this point to Eve, an idea that Dante finds singularly unappealing); that his first word was *El*, a

Hebrew name of God; that it was addressed to God Himself; that it was spoken as soon as Adam was created; and that all this happened wherever Creation itself took place (a point then still in dispute in scholastic commentary on Genesis).

These questions occupy I. iv and v; I. vi is devoted to the slightly thornier question of exactly what language it was that Adam spoke. After reviewing the possibilities, and rejecting the petty linguistic parochialism that has led others to claim that their own native tongue, whatever it may have been, was also Adam's, Dante concludes that Adam in fact spoke Hebrew, and that that language, divinely created and incorruptible, was spoken by all his descendants, until human folly and presumption brought about their linguistic downfall at the Tower of Babel. Later in life he was to modify this view, as the encounter between the protagonist of the *Comedy* and Adam himself, in canto XXVI of *Paradiso*, makes clear; in the later text (*Par.*, XXVI. 124–6), Adam declares that the language he spoke died out even before the disaster of Babel befell the world. (The most obvious consequence of the change is to make even sharper the distinction between the pre- and post-lapsarian condition of both humanity and language; and thus, as we shall see below, to tie the question of linguistic diversity even more closely to that of humanity's moral imperfection.)

The story of the Tower of Babel duly occupies *De vulgari eloquentia* I. vii; many of the accretions to the text of Genesis in Dante's version, particularly the depiction of Nimrod as the ill-fated project's chief instigator, are medieval commonplaces, but the idea that after the tower's fall a new language was allotted to each of the different groups of workers who had been engaged in its construction seems to be a twist of Dante's own.

By now Dante has explained what language is and why many various languages exist; the next two chapters bring the story, with somewhat implausible rapidity, from the Tower of Babel down to his own time. The dispersal of humanity that followed the tower's fall led to the settlement of Europe, and the settlers brought with them a threefold vernacular language for which Dante's term is *ydioma tripharium* (I. viii). Each of this language's three varieties was and is spoken in a particular geographical area: roughly speaking these correspond to Northern, Southern, and Eastern Europe. The variety spoken in Southern Europe is itself tripartite, and its three divisions can be identified by the word each uses as an affirmative: *oc, oïl*, or *sì*. Each of these is used in a particular and well-defined region – to speak roughly once more, in Provence, North-Central France, and Italy,

respectively. It is with these three languages – and overwhelmingly with the language of *sì*, identifiable with Italian (though Dante never actually calls it that) – that the rest of the book will be concerned. Historians of linguistics have frequently seen Dante's account as one of the earliest adumbrations of the concept of the Romance language-group (though recent work by Marcel Danesi provides a cogent critique of this view).

The unfolding tale of humanity's degeneration from linguistic unity (and thus perfection) to its polar opposite – a world that is imperfect because multilingual, and multilingual because imperfect – provokes both serious consideration and a change of argumentative direction in *De vulgari eloquentia* I. ix. In a few pages of immense interest, Dante sums up the whole question of linguistic change across both time and place, displaying a sophisticated and subtle understanding of the process that, once again, marks him out from any of his contemporaries or predecessors. He begins from the obvious and undeniable fact of linguistic diversity in the world, of which he gives several intriguing examples to show that it exists not just among nations, regions, or cities, but even within the boundaries of a single city, such as Bologna; and he then goes on to argue that the existence of this vast range of linguistic phenomena can be attributed to a single underlying cause.

That cause is the fallen state of humanity. Even after Adam and Eve's expulsion from Eden, human beings continued to speak the divinely ordained language that had been spoken by their first ancestors; but the language reconstituted after the calamity at Babel was necessarily inferior to its forerunner – this was our punishment – and its inferiority, in accordance with the standard medieval idea, took the form of increased variety. The existence of numerous languages and the fact that they do not remain constant in either space or time are both, then, signs of the inescapable lack of stability and perfection in human affairs, subject in this as in all things to change, and thus to decay. Dante lays particular stress on the fact of temporal alteration in individual languages. He argues that change of this kind is slow and infinitesimal enough to pass unnoticed within the span of a single lifetime, which makes people unwilling to believe that it happens at all; but, for all that, it is as real as the process that brings a human individual, gradually but inexorably, from youth to maturity – and thence, by implication, to old age. The metaphor is at once striking and illuminating; his sense of the vernacular as a *living* organism, destined to grow, adapt, and one day fade away (rather than as a timelessly rigid system or

immutable set of rules), is another aspect of Dante's linguistic thought that was to find an echo in twentieth-century thinking about language.

From these historical, philosophical, and theological questions Dante turns, in *De vulgari eloquentia* I. x, to matters of (linguistic) geography. In this and the succeeding five chapters he takes his reader on a dialectologist's holiday tour of the Italian peninsula, listing, evaluating, and giving concrete examples of fourteen major and several other minor versions of the Italian vernacular, and making it clear that, in so doing, he is barely scratching the surface of the available material. But although these chapters, as documents of linguistic history, are informative and even entertaining – Dante's disdain for the aesthetic (and moral) shortcomings of most of the vernaculars with which he deals is expressed with a highly agreeable vigour and pungency – their purpose is both broader and more serious. It brings us, indeed, to the core of the *De vulgari eloquentia*, and in some ways also to that of Dante's thinking as a whole.

The tenth chapter of Book I begins, in fact, with a double classification of the three vernaculars of Southern Europe (those of *oc, oïl*, and *sì*), first according to their closeness to their immediate linguistic ancestor (Latin), and then, more significantly, according to the type of literature to which each is best suited. Dante associates the language of *oïl* with prose (which he, conventionally for his time, valued less highly than poetry), and that of *oc* with the poetry of an admirable but long-vanished generation – the troubadours. For these reasons he places both on the lower rungs of his scale; for him the language used by the very best poets in his own day is that of *sì* – the vernacular of Italy. So the search undertaken in *De vulgari eloquentia* I. xi–xv is not just for the most useful, or even the most decorative, form of Italian used in everyday life; it is for the form of the vernacular best adapted to the needs of poetry.

From this point onwards in the *De vulgari eloquentia*, the theorist and historian of language begins to yield to the practitioner of poetic art; or rather, theory and history are progressively absorbed into the poet's intellectual armoury, in order to give him a fuller understanding of what he, as poet, is trying to do. But there is more to it than that. The poet also has a crucial role in the forging of a vernacular whose power and resonance extend beyond the bounds of poetry itself, even beyond any purely artistic conception of poetic language, into direct engagement with the agonies and ambiguities of life in the world. Dante sets out on a hunt – the metaphor is his, first appearing in I. xi – for a verna-

cular that will both answer the needs of the poet as such and fill the intellectual and moral void created at the heart of Italian culture by the absence of a single focal point of political authority in the peninsula – a court. And his failure to find a vernacular that satisfies his requirements has much to do, as the remainder of Book I will show, precisely with that absence.

It is only now – in *De vulgari eloquentia* I. xvi – that the full import of Dante's developing argument becomes clear. His concerns here are as much political as poetic; the language for which he has hunted in vain up and down the Italian peninsula is to be employed for the redemption of Italy's secular institutions as well as for the revitalisation of its poetic traditions. But, as the roll-call of unsatisfactory vernaculars in I. xi–xv makes all too sadly plain, that language does not yet exist – unless Dante himself is to create and define it. And that is what the *De vulgari eloquentia* sets out to do.

This is the most important issue so far raised in the *De vulgari eloquentia*, and it is not by chance that, as Dante's abiding preoccupations with language, poetry and politics emerge, for the first time in this text, in all their inseparably entwined complexity (I. xvi), the linguistic and intellectual difficulty of his argument also reaches levels not previously attained in the course of the work. This single chapter repays close reading and re-reading, both for the lucidity of Dante's thinking and because here he coins the vocabulary and lays down the standards that will underpin his conception of the 'illustrious vernacular' in the remainder of Book I, as well as the foreshortened attempt to exemplify its use in Book II.

The vernacular which Dante has sought and failed to find, then, will be 'illustrious' (I. xvii), 'cardinal', 'aulic', and 'curial' (I. xviii). Dante's explanations of these unusual adjectives are notable for the frequency with which they draw on the rhetoric of politics, consistently interpreting linguistic issues and aesthetic judgements in essentially political terms. (Both 'aulic' and 'curial', of course, have an immediate etymological derivation from the names of political institutions [Latin *aula* and *curia*], but even the more generic word 'illustrious' is explicitly connected by Dante with the honours available to successful politicians rather than with any more obviously poetic conception.) Throughout, the argument intimately connects the idea of the political pre-eminence possessed by a court with that of the poetic supremacy to be enjoyed by the 'illustrious vernacular'; the best in the one sphere requires, of necessity, the best in the other. And, as the last chapter of Book I reveals, the 'illustrious vernacular', like the court, must exert an authority that

extends over the whole community; it is not to be identifiable with the dialect of a single town or region, but must be accessible to all speakers of any other – lesser – variety of the Italian vernacular. Along with the attempt to define the language of the poet, then, goes the desire to establish the language of a nation.

Book II of the *De vulgari eloquentia* is more narrowly focused than Book I, but still flows logically from it. It is also, perhaps, lucid and compact enough to stand in less need of paraphrase or interpretation. It begins from the exact point at which its predecessor ends: having stated the (poetic and political) need for an illustrious vernacular in Italy, and having sought it in vain among either the everyday speeches or the existing poetries of the peninsula, Dante will now set out to show how the ideal language he envisages will be adapted, in practice, to the nature and requirements of lyric poetry. The internal logic of his treatise thus continues its progression from the general to the particular, from the themes of enormous scope that were its starting-point (I. ii–iii), through the sweeping historical and geographical treatments of I. iv–ix, to the specific situation of Italy (I. x–xv) and the as yet elusive vernacular that is its due (I. xvi–xix). We have come a long way – downwards – from the lofty abstractions with which we began; but one of the strengths of Dante's conception is that even the minutiae in which Book II substantially deals are successfully integrated into an overarching scheme of impeccable rigour and coherence. Though judgement must remain provisional – because the book is unfinished – the *De vulgari eloquentia* as it stands gives us no reason to feel that Dante is in anything other than complete command of his material and its exposition. This, of course, only serves to increase the sense of loss that its abbreviated state inspires.

The remaining chapters of Book II are dedicated to the art of poetic composition, seen through the eyes of an acknowledged expert, one who can cite his own works in illustration of his critical points, alongside those of the most distinguished poets of his own and a slightly earlier generation. This is not purely literary criticism in the modern sense, although judgements recognisable as critical certainly form part of Dante's argument; nor is it simply an encyclopedia of poetic terminology or a 'how-to' book for the aspirant to poetic laurels. (The text makes it very clear indeed that by no means all poets will be capable of understanding, let alone practising, the illustrious vernacular in its highest form.) Book II of the *De vulgari eloquentia* fuses Dante's didactic, encyclopaedic, and evaluative interests in poetry, to produce an exhaustive examination (as far as it goes) of the technical aspects of lyric com-

position, but one that also pronounces definitively hostile verdicts on the overwhelming majority of the poetic phenomena with which it deals. Throughout Book II, whether he is discussing metrical forms (*canzone*, sonnet, *ballata*; ii. iii), styles (tragic, elegiac, comic; ii. iv), types of line (hendecasyllable, heptasyllable, pentasyllable; ii. v), levels of 'construction' (flavourless, flavoured, graceful and flavoured, graceful, flavoured and striking; ii. vi), categories of word (infantile, womanish, virile, rustic, urbane, combed, glossy, shaggy, unkempt; ii. vii), or the ways in which all these elements may be combined to create either a whole *canzone* (ii. viii) or an individual stanza (ii. ix–xii), Dante's definitions, arguments and critical opinions are based firmly on two unshakable principles, according to which most of his material is eventually found wanting: hierarchy and appropriateness.

The central importance of hierarchy in Dante's scheme of things will be familiar to anyone who comes to the *De vulgari eloquentia* from a reading of the *Comedy*; and the idea was, of course, so pervasive in medieval culture as a whole that it need be no surprise to find it so clearly exemplified in *De vulgari eloquentia* ii. For every category discussed in ii. iii–vii it is made quite explicit that some kinds – of poem, line, style, construction, word – are, axiomatically and inappellably, *better* than others; and, by extension, it becomes clear that a significant part of the poet's duty is to know how to make such distinctions, and then to cherish them faithfully in his own compositional practice. But – as also in the *Comedy* – the seeming austerity of this principle is tempered by the equal importance of appropriateness. Different kinds are suited to different ends; what is good for the composition of a *canzone* is not necessarily good when writing a sonnet, and a word fit for one particular poetic situation may be disastrously unsuitable for another. The right word in the right place will be right, according to the principle of appropriateness, even when it remains inferior to another word according to the principle of hierarchy. But to replace the inferior but appropriate word with a superior but inappropriate one would not improve the poem – quite the reverse. Both conditions must be satisfied, in every word of every line, before any poem can be deemed a success.

What looks at first like a fussily inflexible and dogmatic preoccupation with minute detail in Book II frequently turns out, instead, to be a sensitive and tolerant scheme that admits and respects the diversity of both means and ends that exists in the realm of vernacular poetic practice. Neither Dante's urgent concern with the 'best' kind of poetry nor his belief that he himself is the poet most qualified and likely to produce it – a belief highlighted rather than obscured by his repeated use of peri-

phrasis to avoid bringing his own name into the argument (I. ix, I. xvii, II. ii, II. v, II. vi) – leads him to pronounce anathema on other kinds of poetry or their characteristic language (though some individual – rival? – poets do come in for the occasional flick of the critical whip). Every variety of poem, every word in the language, is fine in its place. And it may well be that if Dante had carried out his stated intention to discuss levels and styles of poetic art with which the 'illustrious vernacular' could avowedly have nothing to do – the comic, for instance – a completed *De vulgari eloquentia* would have forced us to see the various categories and the relationships among them in a different, clearer, light. This is yet one more reason to regret that the work we have peters out in II. xiv, not only in mid-chapter but in mid-sentence – leaving so exhilarating a project, so interesting a beginning, so vast a territory before both author and reader. The suspicion that, had the *De vulgari eloquentia* been longer, we might never have had the *Comedy* at all, offers at best a shred of consolation.

Select bibliography

The indispensable starting-point for study of the *De vulgari eloquentia* at the close of the twentieth century is provided by two monumental contributions from Pier Vincenzo Mengaldo: his critical edition of the text (Padua, 1968), and the magnificently annotated parallel-text edition, with Italian translation, in Dante Alighieri, *Opere minori*, II· (Milan and Naples, 1979). Mengaldo was also responsible for the comprehensive entry on the *De vulgari eloquentia* in volume II of the *Enciclopedia Dantesca* (Rome, 1970–9), which, along with its ample bibliography, gives an excellent synthetic account of the work's history, contents, manuscript tradition, critical fortunes, contemporary importance, and intellectual substance.

The most important alternative to Mengaldo's parallel-text edition is that of Aristide Marigo (Florence, 1938; third edition, with an appendix by Pier Giorgio Ricci, 1957).

Among other significant scholarly writings in Italian on the *De vulgari eloquentia* are the following:

Baldelli, Ignazio, 'Sulla teoria linguistica di Dante', *Cultura e scuola*, 13–14 (1965): 705–13

Billanovich, Giuseppe, 'Nella tradizione del *De vulgari eloquentia*', in *Prime ricerche dantesche* (Rome, 1947), pp. 13–19

Di Capua, Francesco, *Insegnamenti retorici medievali e dottrine estetiche moderne nel 'De vulgari eloquentia' di Dante* (Naples, 1945); reprinted in *Scritti minori*, vol. III (Rome, 1959), pp. 252–355

Favati, Guido, 'Osservazioni sul *De vulgari eloquentia*', *Annali della Facoltà di Lettere, Filosofia e Magistero dell'Università di Cagliari*, 29 (1961–5): 151–213

Nardi, Bruno, 'Il linguaggio', in *Dante e la cultura medievale*, new edn (Bari, 1983), pp. 173–95 (first published 1942)

Pagani, Ileana, *La teoria linguistica di Dante: 'De vulgari eloquentia': discussioni, scelte, proposte* (Naples, 1982)

Peirone, Luigi, *Il 'De vulgari eloquentia' e la linguistica moderna* (Genoa, 1975)

Schiaffini, Alfredo, *Interpretazione del 'De vulgari eloquentia' di Dante* (Rome, 1963)

Vinay, Gustavo, 'Ricerche sul *De vulgari eloquentia*', *Giornale storico della letteratura italiana*, 136 (1959): 237–74, 367–88

'La teoria linguistica del *De vulgari eloquentia*', *Cultura e scuola*, 5 (1962): 30–42

The following works in English were found especially useful during the preparation of the present translation:

Ascoli, Albert Russell, ' "Neminem ante nos": History and Authority in the *De vulgari eloquentia*', *Annali d'Italianistica*, 8 (1990): 186–231

Barański, Zygmunt G., 'Divine, Human and Animal Languages in Dante: Notes on *De vulgari eloquentia* i.i–ix and the Bible', *Transactions of the Philological Society*, 87 (1989): 205–31

Cestaro, Gary P., ' "...quanquam Sarnum biberimus ante dentes...": The Primal Scene of Suckling in Dante's *De vulgari eloquentia*', *Dante Studies*, 109 (1991): 119–47

Cremona, Joseph, 'Dante's Views on Language', in *The Mind of Dante*, edited by U. Limentani (Cambridge, 1965), pp. 138–62

Danesi, Marcel, 'Latin vs Romance in the Middle Ages: Dante's *De vulgari eloquentia* Revisited', in *Latin and the Romance Languages in the Early Middle Ages*, edited by Roger Wright (London and New York, 1991), pp. 248–58

Dronke, Peter, 'Excursus I', in *Dante and Medieval Latin Traditions* (Cambridge, 1986), pp. 103–11

Grayson, Cecil, ' "*Nobilior est vulgaris*": Latin and Vernacular in Dante's Thought', in *Centenary Essays on Dante by Members of the Oxford Dante Society* (Oxford, 1965), pp. 54–76

Shapiro, Marianne, '*De vulgari eloquentia*: Dante's Book of Exile' (Lincoln, USA, and London, 1990)

Welliver, Warman, *Dante in Hell: The 'De vulgari eloquentia'* (Ravenna, 1981)

Yowell, Donna L., 'Human Speech and Bestial Silence: *De vulgari eloquentia* in *Inferno* XXXI–XXXIV', Ph.D. diss., University of California at Berkeley, 1987.

A note on the text

With a single exception – 'speculationem' for 'locutionem' in I. iii.I, discussed in the notes – I have followed the text of Mengaldo's 1968 edition (correcting the obvious misprint 'nal' for 'nam' in I. ix. 2). As stated in the Introduction above, the textual history of the *De vulgari eloquentia* is comparatively straightforward, with the oldest manuscript, B, being accepted as the most authoritative witness to the tradition by all modern editors, and forming the basis of both the major critical editions of the last sixty years. Between Mengaldo and his most illustrious twentieth-century rival, Marigo, I have found only a few genuinely significant differences of reading (in the Latin – Marigo freely 'corrects' Dante's vernacular quotations, Mengaldo is much more conservative). All these are duly signalled in the notes. (Merely orthographical variations, such as Marigo's 'haurientes' for 'aurientes' in I. i. I, are not so signalled; neither are different orderings of identical words, such as Marigo's 'redactum sive inventum est' for 'redactum est sive inventum' in I. x. 2.) In most of the substantially different cases, Mengaldo (1968 and 1979) seems to me clearly preferable; in one, however, – I. iii, the exception mentioned above – Mengaldo (1979) silently corrects Mengaldo (1968) and reverts to Marigo's reading. Punctuation and paragraphing are those of Mengaldo (1968); Mengaldo's later edition shows many alterations in this regard, but none strikes me as compelling.

De vulgari eloquentia

Liber Primus

I

1   Cum neminem ante nos de vulgaris eloquentie doctrina quicquam inveniamus tractasse, atque talem scilicet eloquentiam penitus omnibus necessariam videamus, cum ad eam non tantum viri sed etiam mulieres et parvuli nitantur, in quantum natura permictit; volentes discretionem aliqualiter lucidare illorum qui tanquam ceci ambulant per plateas, plerunque anteriora posteriora putantes, Verbo aspirante de celis locutioni vulgarium gentium prodesse temptabimus, non solum aquam nostri ingenii ad tantum poculum aurientes, sed, accipiendo vel compilando ab aliis, potiora miscentes, ut exinde potionare possimus dulcissimum ydromellum.

2   Sed quia unamquanque doctrinam oportet non probare, sed suum aperire subiectum, ut sciatur quid sit super quod illa versatur, dicimus, celeriter actendentes, quod vulgarem locutionem appellamus eam qua infantes assuefiunt ab assistentibus cum primitus distinguere voces incipiunt; vel, quod brevius dici potest, vulgarem locutionem asserimus 3 quam sine omni regula nutricem imitantes accipimus. Est et inde alia locutio secundaria nobis, quam Romani gramaticam vocaverunt. Hanc quidem secundariam Greci habent et alii, sed non omnes: ad habitum vero huius pauci perveniunt, quia non nisi per spatium temporis et studii assiduitatem regulamur et doctrinamur in illa.

4   Harum quoque duarum nobilior est vulgaris: tum quia prima fuit humano generi usitata; tum quia totus orbis ipsa perfruitur, licet in diversas prolationes et vocabula sit divisa; tum quia naturalis est nobis, cum illa potius artificialis existat.

5   Et de hac nobiliori nostra est intentio pertractare.

Book One

I

Since I find that no one, before myself, has dealt in any way with the 1
theory of eloquence in the vernacular, and since we can plainly see that
such eloquence is necessary to everyone – for not only men, but also
women and children strive to acquire it, as far as nature allows – I shall
try, inspired by the Word that comes from above, to say something useful
about the language of people who speak the vulgar tongue, hoping
thereby to enlighten somewhat the understanding of those who walk
the streets like the blind, ever thinking that what lies ahead is behind
them. Yet, in so doing, I shall not bring to so large a cup only the water of
my own thinking, but shall add to it more potent ingredients, taken or ex-
tracted from elsewhere, so that from these I may concoct the sweetest
possible mead.

But since it is required of any theoretical treatment that it not leave 2
its basis implicit, but declare it openly, so that it may be clear with what
its argument is concerned, I say, hastening to deal with the question,
that I call 'vernacular language' that which infants acquire from those
around them when they first begin to distinguish sounds; or, to put it
more succinctly, I declare that vernacular language is that which we
learn without any formal instruction, by imitating our nurses. There 3
also exists another kind of language, at one remove from us, which the
Romans called *gramatica*.[1] The Greeks and some – but not all – other
peoples also have this secondary kind of language. Few, however,
achieve complete fluency in it, since knowledge of its rules and theory
can only be developed through dedication to a lengthy course of
study.

Of these two kinds of language, the more noble is the vernacular: 4
first, because it was the language originally used by the human race;
second, because the whole world employs it, though with different pro-
nunciations and using different words; and third, because it is natural to
us, while the other is, in contrast, artificial.

And this more noble kind of language is what I intend to discuss. 5

3

II

1 Hec est nostrà vera prima locutio. Non dico autem 'nostra' ut et aliam sit esse locutionem quam hominis: nam eorum que sunt omnium soli
2 homini datum est loqui, cum solum sibi necessarium fuerit. Non angelis, non inferioribus animalibus necessarium fuit loqui, sed nequicquam datum fuisset eis: quod nempe facere natura aborret.
3 Si etenim perspicaciter consideramus quid cum loquimur intendamus, patet quod nichil aliud quam nostre mentis enucleare aliis conceptum. Cum igitur angeli ad pandendas gloriosas eorum conceptiones habeant promptissimam atque ineffabilem sufficientiam intellectus, qua vel alter alteri totaliter innotescit per se, vel saltim per illud fulgentissimum Speculum in quo cuncti representantur pulcerrimi atque avidis-
4 simi speculantur, nullo signo locutionis indiguisse videntur. Et si obiciatur de hiis qui corruerunt spiritibus, dupliciter responderi potest: primo quod, cum de hiis que necessaria sunt ad bene esse tractemus, eos preterire debemus, cum divinam curam perversi expectare noluerunt; secundo et melius quod ipsi demones ad manifestandam inter se perfidiam suam non indigent nisi ut sciat quilibet de quolibet quia est et quantus est; quod quidem sciunt: cognoverunt enim se invicem ante ruinam suam.
5 Inferioribus quoque animalibus, cum solo nature instinctu ducantur, de locutione non oportuit provideri: nam omnibus eiusdem speciei sunt iidem actus et passiones, et sic possunt per proprios alienos cognoscere; inter ea vero que diversarum sunt specierum non solum non necessaria fuit locutio, sed prorsus dampnosa fuisset, cum nullum amicabile commertium fuisset in illis.
6 Et si obiciatur de serpente loquente ad primam mulierem, vel de asina Balaam, quod locuti sint, ad hoc respondemus quod angelus in illa et dyabolus in illo taliter operati sunt quod ipsa animalia moverunt organa sua, sic ut vox inde resultavit distincta tanquam vera locutio; non quod aliud esset asine illud quam rudere, neque quam sibilare ser-
7 penti. Si vero contra argumentetur quis de eo quod Ovidius dicit in quinto Metamorfoseos de picis loquentibus, dicimus quod hoc figurate dicit, aliud intelligens. Et si dicatur quod pice adhuc et alie aves locuntur, dicimus quod falsum est, quia talis actus locutio non est, sed quedam imitatio soni nostre vocis; vel quod nituntur imitari nos in quantum sonamus, sed non in quantum loquimur. Unde si expresse dicenti 'pica' resonaret etiam 'pica', non esset hec nisi representatio vel imitatio soni illius qui prius dixisset.

II

This, in truth, is our primary language. I do not, though, say 'our' 1
because there is or could be any other kind of language than that of
human beings; for, of all creatures that exist, only human beings were
given the power of speech, because only to them was it necessary. It was 2
not necessary that either angels or the lower animals should be able to
speak; rather, this power would have been wasted on them, and nature,
of course, hates to do anything superfluous.[2]

Now, if we wish to define with precision what our intention is when 3
we speak, it is clearly nothing other than to expound to others the con-
cepts formed in our minds. Therefore, since the angels possess, in order to
communicate their own glorious conceptions, a ready and ineffable suffi-
ciency of intellect – through which either they make themselves, in
themselves, completely known to each other, or, at least, are reflected, in
the fullness of their beauty and ardour, by that resplendent mirror which
retains an image of all of them – they seem not to have needed signs to re-
present speech. And if it be objected that some angels have fallen from 4
heaven, a twofold answer may be made. First, that when we are dis-
cussing things that are necessary for a rightly ordered life, we should
leave the fallen angels aside, since, in their perversity, they chose not to
wait on God's care; second, and better, that these demons, in order to de-
monstrate their corruption to each other, need only to know, of any one of
their number, the nature and the degree of his fallen condition. And this
they already know, for they knew each other before their ruin.

As for the lower animals, since they are guided only by their natural 5
instinct, it was not necessary for them to be given the power of speech.
For all animals that belong to the same species are identical in respect of
action and feeling; and thus they can know the actions and feelings of
others by knowing their own. Between creatures of different species, on
the other hand, not only was speech unnecessary, but it would have been
injurious, since there could have been no friendly exchange between
them.

And if it be objected that the serpent addressed the first woman, or 6
that the ass did likewise to Balaam, and that they did so by speaking, I
reply that an angel (in the latter case) and the devil (in the former)
brought it about that the animals in question manipulated their vocal
organs in such a way that a sound came out that resembled real speech;
but to the ass this was nothing more than braying, to the serpent, only
hissing.[3] Moreover, if anyone finds a contrary argument in what Ovid, 7

8   Et sic patet soli homini datum fuisse loqui. Sed quare necessarium sibi foret, breviter pertractare conemur.

III

1   Cum igitur homo non nature instinctu, sed ratione moveatur, et ipsa ratio vel circa discretionem vel circa iudicium vel circa electionem diversificetur in singulis, adeo ut fere quilibet sua propria specie videatur gaudere, per proprios actus vel passiones, ut brutum animal, neminem alium intelligere opinamur. Nec per spiritualem speculationem, ut angelum, alterum alterum introire contingit, cum grossitie atque opacitate mortalis corporis humanus spiritus sit obtectus.

2   Oportuit ergo genus humanum ad comunicandas inter se conceptiones suas aliquod rationale signum et sensuale habere: quia, cum de ratione accipere habeat et in rationem portare, rationale esse oportuit; cumque de una ratione in aliam nichil deferri possit nisi per medium sensuale, sensuale esse oportuit. Quare, si tantum rationale esset, pertransire non posset; si tantum sensuale, nec a ratione accipere nec in rationem deponere potuisset.

3   Hoc equidem signum est ipsum subiectum nobile de quo loquimur: nam sensuale quid est in quantum sonus est; rationale vero in quantum aliquid significare videtur ad placitum.

IV

1   Soli homini datum fuit ut loqueretur, ut ex premissis manifestum est. Nunc quoque investigandum esse existimo cui hominum primum

in the fifth book of the *Metamorphoses*, says about talking magpies, I reply that this is said figuratively, and means something else.[4] And if it be claimed that, to this day, magpies and other birds do indeed speak, I say that this is not so; for their act is not speaking, but rather an imitation of the sound of the human voice – or it may be that they try to imitate us in so far as we make a noise, but not in so far as we speak. So that, if to someone who said '*pica*'[5] aloud the bird were to return the word '*pica*', this would only be a reproduction or imitation of the sound made by the person who uttered the word first.

And so it is clear that the power of speech was given only to human   8 beings. But now I shall try briefly to investigate why it should have been necessary for them.

III

Since, therefore, human beings are moved not by their natural instinct   1 but by reason, and since that reason takes diverse forms in individuals, according to their capacity for discrimination, judgement, or choice – to the point where it appears that almost everyone enjoys the existence of a unique species – I hold that we can never understand the actions or feelings of others by reference to our own, as the baser animals can. Nor is it given to us to enter into each other's minds by means of spiritual reflection,[6] as the angels do, because the human spirit is so weighed down[7] by the heaviness and density of the mortal body.

So it was necessary that the human race, in order for its members to   2 communicate their conceptions among themselves, should have some signal based on reason and perception. Since this signal needed to receive its content from reason and convey it back there, it had to be rational; but, since nothing can be conveyed from one reasoning mind to another except by means perceptible to the senses, it had also to be based on perception. For, if it were purely rational, it could not make its journey; if purely perceptible, it could neither derive anything from reason nor deliver anything to it.

This signal, then, is the noble foundation that I am discussing;[8] for it   3 is perceptible, in that it is a sound, and yet also rational, in that this sound, according to convention, is taken to mean something.

IV

So the power of speech was given only to human beings, as is plain   1 from what was said above. I think it now also incumbent upon me to find

locutio data sit, et quid primitus locutus fuerit, et ad quem, et ubi, et quando, nec non et sub quo ydiomate primiloquium emanavit.

2   Secundum quidem quod in principio Genesis loquitur, ubi de primordio mundi Sacratissima Scriptura pertractat, mulierem invenitur ante omnes fuisse locutam, scilicet presumptuosissimam Evam, cum dyabolo sciscitanti respondit: 'De fructu lignorum que sunt in paradiso vescimur; de fructu vero ligni quod est in medio paradisi precepit nobis
3   Deus ne comederemus nec tangeremus, ne forte moriamur'. Sed quanquam mulier in scriptis prius inveniatur locuta, rationabilius tamen est ut hominem prius locutum fuisse credamus, et inconvenienter putatur tam egregium humani generis actum non prius a viro quam a femina profluxisse. Rationabiliter ergo credimus ipsi Ade prius datum fuisse loqui ab Eo qui statim ipsum plasmaverat.

4   Quid autem prius vox primi loquentis sonaverit, viro sane mentis in promptu esse non titubo ipsum fuisse quod 'Deus' est, scilicet El, vel per modum interrogationis vel per modum responsionis. Absurdum atque rationi videtur orrificum ante Deum ab homine quicquam nominatum fuisse, cum ab ipso et in ipsum factus fuisset homo. Nam sicut post prevaricationem humani generis quilibet exordium sue locutionis incipit ab 'heu', rationabile est quod ante qui fuit inciperet a gaudio; et cum nullum gaudium sit extra Deum, sed totum in Deo, et ipse Deus totus sit gaudium, consequens est quod primus loquens primo et ante omnia dixisset 'Deus'.

5   Oritur et hinc ista questio, cum dicimus superius per via responsionis hominem primum fuisse locutum, si responsio fuit ad Deum: nam, si ad Deum fuit, iam videretur quod Deus locutus extitisset, quod contra
6   superius prelibata videtur insurgere. Ad quod quidem dicimus quod bene potuit respondisse Deo interrogante, nec propter hoc Deus locutus est ipsa quam dicimus locutionem. Quis enim dubitat quicquid est ad Dei nutum esse flexibile, quo quidem facta, quo conservata, quo etiam gubernata sunt omnia? Igitur cum ad tantas alterationes moveatur aer imperio nature inferioris, que ministra et factura Dei est, ut tonitrua personet, ignem fulgoret, aquam gemat, spargat nivem, grandines lancinet, nonne imperio Dei movebitur ad quedam sonare verba, ipso distinguente qui maiora distinxit? Quid ni?
7   Quare ad hoc et ad quedam alia hec sufficere credimus.

out to which human being that power was first granted, and what he first said, and to,whom, and where, and when; and also in what language that primal utterance was made.

According to what it says at the beginning of Genesis, where sacred 2 scripture describes the origin of the world, we find that a woman spoke before anyone else, when the most presumptuous Eve responded thus to the blandishments of the Devil: 'We may eat of the fruit of the trees that are in Paradise: but God has forbidden us to eat or to touch the fruit of the tree which is in the middle of Paradise, lest we die.'[9] But although we find 3 in scripture that a woman spoke first, I still think it more reasonable that a man should have done so; and it may be thought unseemly that so distinguished an action of the human race should first have been performed by a woman rather than a man. Therefore it is reasonable to believe that the power of speech was given first to Adam, by Him who had just created him.[10]

As to what was first pronounced by the voice of the first speaker, that 4 will readily be apparent to anyone in their right mind, and I have no doubt that it was the name of God, or *El*, in the form either of a question or of an answer. It is manifestly absurd, and an offence against reason, to think that anything should have been named by a human being before God, when he had been made human by Him and for Him. For if, since the disaster that befell the human race, the speech of every one of us has begun with 'woe!',[11] it is reasonable that he who existed before should have begun with a cry of joy; and, since there is no joy outside God, but all joy is in God, and since God Himself is joy itself, it follows that the first man to speak should first and before all have said 'God'.

From this arises a question: if, as I said above, the first man spoke in 5 the form of an answer, was that answer addressed to God? For if it was, it would seem that God had already spoken – which would appear to raise an objection to the argument offered above.[12] To this, however, I reply 6 that Adam may well have answered a question from God; nor, on that account, need God have spoken using what we would call language. For who doubts that everything that exists obeys a sign from God, by whom, indeed, all things are created, preserved, and, finally, maintained in order? Therefore, if the air can be moved, at the command of the lesser nature which is God's servant and creation, to transformations so profound that thunderbolts crash, lightning flashes, waters rage, snow falls, and hailstones fly, can it not also, at God's command, so be moved as to make the sound of words, if He distinguishes them who has made much greater distinctions? Why not?

V

1   Opinantes autem non sine ratione, tam ex superioribus quam inferioribus sumpta, ad ipsum Deum primitus primum hominem direxisse locutionem, rationabiliter dicimus ipsum loquentem primum, mox postquam afflatus est ab Animante Virtute, incunctanter fuisse locutum. Nam in homine sentiri humanius credimus quam sentire, dummodo sentiatur et sentiat tanquam homo. Si ergo Faber ille atque Perfectionis Principium et Amator afflando primum nostrum omni perfectione complevit, rationabile nobis apparet nobilissimum animal non ante sentire quam sentiri cepisse.

2   Si quis vero fatetur contra obiciens quod non oportebat illum loqui, cum solus adhuc homo existeret, et Deus omnia sine verbis archana nostra discernat etiam ante quam nos, cum illa reverentia dicimus, qua uti oportet cum de Eterna Voluntate aliquid iudicamus, quod licet Deus sciret, immo presciret (quod idem est quantum ad Deum) absque locutione conceptum primi loquentis, voluit tamen et ipsum loqui, ut in explicatione tante dotis gloriaretur ipse qui gratis dotaverat. Et ideo divinitus in nobis esse credendum est quod in actu nostrorum effectuum ordinato letamur.

3   Et hinc penitus elicere possumus locum illum ubi effutita est prima locutio: quoniam, si extra paradisum afflatus est homo, extra, si vero intra, intra fuisse locum prime locutionis convicimus.

VI

1   Quoniam permultis ac diversis ydiomatibus negotium exercitatur humanum, ita quod multi multis non aliter intelligantur verbis quam sine verbis, de ydiomate illo venari nos decet quo vir sine matre, vir sine lacte, qui nec pupillarem etatem nec vidit adultam, creditur usus.

2   In hoc, sicut etiam in multis aliis, Petramala civitas amplissima est, et patria maiori parti filiorum Adam. Nam quicunque tam obscene rationis est ut locum sue nationis delitiosissimum credat esse sub sole, hic etiam pre cunctis proprium vulgare licetur, idest maternam locutionem,

On this account, I think that such an answer is adequate for both 7
this and other questions.

V

Thinking, therefore, not without reasonable grounds derived both 1
from above and from below,[13] that the first man addressed his first speech
to God Himself, I say, equally reasonably, that this first speaker spoke im-
mediately – as soon, indeed, as God's creative power had been breathed
into him. For we hold that it is more truly human for a human being to be
perceived than to perceive, as long as he or she is perceived and perceives
as a human being. So if our creator, that source and lover of perfection,
completed our first ancestor by infusing all perfection into him, I find it
reasonable that this most noble creature should not have begun to per-
ceive before he was perceived.

If, though, someone should object to this, saying that there was no 2
need for him to speak, since he was the only human being yet in exis-
tence, and since God knows all our secrets without our putting them into
words (indeed, before we know them ourselves), I reply, with all the rever-
ence that we must feel when expressing an opinion about the eternal will
of God, that even if God knew (or rather foreknew, which is the same
thing where God is concerned) the first speaker's conception without his
having to speak, yet He still wished that Adam should speak, so that He
who had freely given so great a gift should be glorified in its employment.
And likewise, we must believe that the fact that we rejoice in the ordered
activity of our faculties is a sign of divinity in us.

And from this we can confidently deduce where the first speech was 3
uttered: for I have clearly shown that, if God's spirit was breathed into
man outside Paradise, then it was outside Paradise that he spoke; if
indeed inside, then the place of the first speech was in Paradise itself.[14]

VI

Since human affairs are now carried on in so many different lan- 1
guages, so that many people are no better understood by others when
they use words than when they do not, it behoves us to hunt for the lan-
guage believed to have been used by the man who never had a mother nor
drank her milk, the man who never saw either childhood or maturity.[15]

In this, as in many other matters, Pietramala[16] is a great city indeed, 2
the home of the greater part of the children of Adam. For whoever is so
misguided as to think that the place of his birth is the most delightful spot

3   et per consequens credit ipsum fuisse illud quod fuit Ade. Nos autem,
cui mundus est patria velut piscibus equor, quanquam Sarnum biber-
imus ante dentes et Florentiam adeo diligamus ut, quia dileximus,
exilium patiamur iniuste, rationi magis quam sensui spatulas nostri
iudicii podiamus. Et quamvis ad voluptatem nostram sive nostre sensua-
litatis quietem in terris amenior locus quam Florentia non existat, revol-
ventes et poetarum et aliorum scriptorum volumina, quibus mundus
universaliter et membratim describitur, ratiocinantesque in nobis situa-
tiones varias mundi locorum et eorum habitudinem ad utrunque polum
et circulum equatorem, multas esse perpendimus firmiterque censemus
et magis nobiles et magis delitiosas et regiones et urbes quam Tusciam et
Florentiam, unde sumus oriundus et civis, et plerasque nationes et
gentes delectabiliori atque utiliori sermone uti quam Latinos.

4   Redeuntes igitur ad propositum, dicimus certam formam locutionis
a Deo cum anima prima concreatam fuisse. Dico autem 'formam' et
quantum ad rerum vocabula et quantum ad vocabulorum construc-
tionem et quantum ad constructionis prolationem; qua quidem forma
omnis lingua loquentium uteretur, nisi culpa presumptionis humane
dissipata fuisset, ut inferius ostendetur.

5   Hac forma locutionis locutus est Adam; hac forma locutionis locuti
sunt omnes posteri eius usque ad edificationem turris Babel, que 'turris
confusionis' interpretatur; hanc formam locutionis hereditati sunt filii
6   Heber, qui ab eo dicti sunt Hebrei. Hiis solis post confusionem remansit,
ut Redemptor noster, qui ex illis oriturus erat secundum humanitatem,
non lingua confusionis, sed gratie frueretur.

7   Fuit ergo hebraicum ydioma illud quod primi loquentis labia fabri-
carunt.

VII

1   Dispudet, heu, nunc humani generis ignominiam renovare! Sed quia
preterire non possumus quin transeamus per illam, quanquam rubor ad
ora consurgat animusque refugiat, percurremus.

2   O semper natura nostra prona peccatis! O ab initio et nunquam desi-
nens nequitatrix! Num fuerat satis ad tui correptionem quod, per
primam prevaricationem eluminata, delitiarum exulabas a patria? Num

under the sun may also believe that his own language – his mother
tongue, that is – is pre-eminent among all others; and, as a result, he may
believe that his language was also Adam's. To me, however, the whole 3
world is a homeland, like the sea to fish – though I drank from the Arno
before cutting my teeth, and love Florence so much that, because I loved
her, I suffer exile unjustly[17] – and I will weight the balance of my judge-
ment more with reason than with sentiment. And although for my own
enjoyment (or rather for the satisfaction of my own desire), there is no
more agreeable place on earth than Florence, yet when I turn the pages
of the volumes of poets and other writers, by whom the world is described
as a whole and in its constituent parts, and when I reflect inwardly on the
various locations of places in the world, and their relations to the two
poles and the circle at the equator, I am convinced, and firmly maintain,
that there are many regions and cities more noble and more delightful
than Tuscany and Florence, where I was born and of which I am a citizen,
and many nations and peoples who speak a more elegant and practical
language than do the Italians.

Returning, then, to my subject, I say that a certain form of language 4
was created by God along with the first soul; I say 'form' with reference
both to the words used for things, and to the construction of words, and
to the arrangement of the construction; and this form of language would
have continued to be used by all speakers, had it not been shattered
through the fault of human presumption, as will be shown below.

In this form of language Adam spoke; in this form of language spoke 5
all his descendants until the building of the Tower of Babel (which is in-
terpreted as 'tower of confusion'); this is the form of language inherited
by the sons of Heber, who are called Hebrews because of it.[18] To these 6
alone it remained after the confusion, so that our redeemer, who was to
descend from them (in so far as He was human), should not speak the lan-
guage of confusion, but that of grace.

So the Hebrew language was that which the lips of the first speaker 7
moulded.[19]

VII

Alas, how it shames me now to recall the dishonouring of the 1
human race! But since I can make no progress without passing that way,
though a blush comes to my cheek and my spirit recoils, I shall make
haste to do so.

Oh human nature, always inclined towards sin! Engaged in evil[20] 2
from the beginning, and never changing your ways! Was it not enough to

satis quod, per universalem familie tue luxuriem et trucitatem, unica re-
servata domo, quicquid tui iuris erat cataclismo perierat, et ‹que› com-
miseras tu animalia celi terreque iam luerant? Quippe satis extiterat.
Sed, sicut proverbialiter dici solet, 'Non ante tertium equitabis', misera
3 miserum venire maluisti ad equum. Ecce, lector, quod vel oblitus homo
vel vilipendens disciplinas priores, et avertens oculos a vibicibus que re-
manserant, tertio insurrexit ad verbera, per superbam stultitiam presu-
mendo.

4 Presumpsit ergo in corde suo incurabilis homo, sub persuasione gi-
gantis Nembroth, arte sua non solum superare naturam, sed etiam
ipsum naturantem, qui Deus est, et cepit edificare turrim in Sennaar, que
postea dicta est Babel, hoc est 'confusio', per quam celum sperabat ascen-
5 dere, intendens inscius non equare, sed suum superare Factorem. O sine
mensura clementia celestis imperii! Quis patrum tot sustineret insultus
a filio? Sed exurgens non hostili scutica sed paterna et alias verberibus
assueta, rebellantem filium pia correctione nec non memorabili casti-
gavit.

6 Siquidem pene totum humanum genus ad opus iniquitatis coierat:
pars imperabant, pars architectabantur, pars muros moliebantur, pars
amussibus regulabant, pars trullis linebant, pars scindere rupes, pars
mari, pars terra vehere intendebant, partesque diverse diversis aliis oper-
ibus indulgebant; cum celitus tanta confusione percussi sunt ut, qui
omnes una eademque loquela deserviebant ad opus, ab opere multis di-
versificati loquelis desinerent et nunquam ad idem commertium conve-
7 nirent. Solis etenim in uno convenientibus actu eadem loquela remansit:
puta cunctis architectoribus una, cunctis saxa volventibus una, cunctis
ea parantibus una; et sic de singulis operantibus accidit. Quot quot
autem exercitii varietates tendebant ad opus, tot tot ydiomatibus tunc
genus humanum disiungitur; et quanto excellentius exercebant, tanto
rudius nunc barbariusque locuntur.

8 Quibus autem sacratum ydioma remansit nec aderant nec exercitium
commendabant, sed graviter detestantes stoliditatem operantium deri-
debant. Sed hec minima pars, quantum ad numerum, fuit de semine
Sem, sicut conicio, qui fuit tertius filius Noe: de qua quidem ortus est
populus Israel, qui antiquissima locutione sunt usi usque ad suam dis-
persionem.

correct you that, banished from the light for the first transgression, you should live in exile from the delights of your homeland? Was it not enough that, because of the all-pervading lust and cruelty of your race, everything that was yours should have perished in a cataclysm, one family alone being spared, and that the creatures of earth and sky should have had to pay for the wrongs that you had committed?[21] It should indeed have been enough. But, as we often say in the form of a proverb, 'not before the third time will you ride';[22] and you, wretched humanity, chose to mount a fractious steed. And so, reader, the human race, either 3 forgetful or disdainful of earlier punishments, and averting its eyes from the bruises that remained, came for a third time to deserve a beating, putting its trust in its own foolish pride.

Incorrigible humanity, therefore, led astray by the giant Nimrod, pre- 4 sumed in its heart to outdo in skill not only nature but the source of its own nature, who is God; and began to build a tower in Sennaar, which afterwards was called Babel (that is, 'confusion').[23] By this means human beings hoped to climb up to heaven, intending in their foolishness not to equal but to excel their creator. Oh boundless mercy of the kingdom of 5 heaven! What other father would have borne so many insults from his child? Yet, rising up not with an enemy's whip but that of a father, already accustomed to dealing out punishment, He chastised His rebellious off- spring with a lesson as holy as it was memorable.

Almost the whole of the human race had collaborated in this work of 6 evil. Some gave orders, some drew up designs; some built walls, some measured them with plumb-lines, some smeared mortar on them with trowels; some were intent on breaking stones, some on carrying them by sea, some by land; and other groups still were engaged in other activities – until they were all struck by a great blow from heaven. Previously all of them had spoken one and the same language while carrying out their tasks; but now they were forced to leave off their labours, never to return to the same occupation, because they had been split up into groups speaking different languages. Only among those who were engaged in a 7 particular activity did their language remain unchanged; so, for in- stance, there was one for all the architects, one for all the carriers of stones, one for all the stone-breakers, and so on for all the different opera- tions. As many as were the types of work involved in the enterprise, so many were the languages by which the human race was fragmented; and the more skill required for the type of work, the more rudimentary and barbaric the language they now spoke.

But the holy tongue remained to those who had neither joined in the 8 project nor praised it, but instead, thoroughly disdaining it, had made

VIII

1   Ex precedenter memorata confusione linguarum non leviter opi-
namur per universa mundi climata climatumque plagas incolendas et
angulos tunc primum homines fuisse dispersos. Et cum radix humane
propaginis principalis in oris orientalibus sit plantata, nec non ab inde ad
utrunque latus per diffusos multipliciter palmites nostra sit extensa
propago, demumque ad fines occidentales protracta, forte primitus tunc
2   vel totius Europe flumina, vel saltim quedam, rationalia guctura pota-
verunt. Sed sive advene tunc primitus advenissent, sive ad Europam indi-
gene repedassent, ydioma secum tripharium homines actulerunt; et
afferentium hoc alii meridionalem, alii septentrionalem regionem in
Europa sibi sortiti sunt; et tertii, quos nunc Grecos vocamus, partim
Europe, partim Asye occuparunt.
3   Ab uno postea eodemque ydiomate in vindice confusione recepto
diversa vulgaria traxerunt originem, sicut inferius ostendemus. Nam
totum quod ab hostiis Danubii sive Meotidis paludibus usque ad fines oc-
cidentales Anglie Ytalorum Francorumque finibus et Oceano limitatur,
solum unum obtinuit ydioma, licet postea per Sclavones, Ungaros, Teuto-
nicos, Saxones, Anglicos et alias nationes quamplures fuerit per diversa
vulgaria dirivatum, hoc solo fere omnibus in signum eiusdem principii
4   remanente, quod quasi predicti omnes *iò* affirmando respondent. Ab isto
incipiens ydiomate, videlicet a finibus Ungarorum versus orientem, aliud
occupavit totum quod ab inde vocatur Europa, nec non ulterius est pro-
tractum.
5   Totum vero quod in Europa restat ab istis tertium tenuit ydioma, licet
nunc tripharium videatur: nam alii *oc*, alii *oïl*, alii *sì* affirmando locuntur,
ut puta Yspani, Franci et Latini. Signum autem quod ab uno eodemque
ydiomate istarum trium gentium progrediantur vulgaria, in promptu
est, quia multa per eadem vocabula nominare videntur, ut 'Deum', 'celum',
6   'amorem', 'mare', 'terram', 'est', 'vivit', 'moritur', 'amat', alia fere omnia.
Istorum vero proferentes *oc* meridionalis Europe tenent partem occiden-
talem, a Ianuensium finibus incipientes. Qui autem *sì* dicunt a predictis
finibus orientalem tenent, videlicet usque ad promuntorium illud Ytalie
qua sinus Adriatici maris incipit, et Siciliam. Sed loquentes *oïl* quodam
modo septentrionales sunt respectu istorum: nam ab oriente Alamannos

fun of the builders' stupidity. This insignificant minority – insignificant in numbers alone – were, as I believe, of the family of Shem, Noah's third son, from which descended the people of Israel, who used this most ancient language until the time of their dispersal.

VIII

The confusion of languages recorded above leads me, on no trivial 1 grounds, to the opinion that it was then that human beings were first scattered throughout the whole world, into every temperate zone and habitable region, right to its furthest corners. And since the principal root from which the human race has grown was planted in the East, and from there our growth has spread, through many branches and in all directions, finally reaching the furthest limits of the West, perhaps it was then that the rivers of all Europe, or at least some of them, first refreshed the throats of rational beings. But, whether they were arriving then for the 2 first time, or whether they had been born in Europe and were now returning there, these people brought with them a tripartite language. Of those who brought it, some found their way to southern Europe and some to northern; and a third group, whom we now call Greeks, settled partly in Europe and partly in Asia.[24]

Later, from this tripartite language (which had been received in that 3 vengeful confusion),[25] different vernaculars developed, as I shall show below. For in that whole area that extends from the mouth of the Danube (or the Meotide marshes)[26] to the westernmost shores of England, and which is defined by the boundaries of the Italians and the French,[27] and by the ocean, only one language prevailed, although later it was split up into many vernaculars by the Slavs, the Hungarians, the Teutons, the Saxons, the English, and several other nations. Only one sign of their common origin remains in almost all of them, namely that nearly all the nations listed above, when they answer in the affirmative, say *iò*. Starting 4 from the furthest point reached by this vernacular (that is, from the boundary of the Hungarians towards the east), another occupied all the rest of what, from there onwards, is called Europe; and it stretches even beyond that.

All the rest of Europe that was not dominated by these two vernacu- 5 lars was held by a third, although nowadays this itself seems to be divided in three: for some now say *oc*, some *oïl*, and some *sì*, when they answer in the affirmative; and these are the Hispanic,[28] the French, and the Italians. Yet the sign that the vernaculars of these three peoples derive from one and the same language is plainly apparent: for they can be seen to use

habent et ab occidente et septentrione anglico mari vallati sunt et montibus Aragonie terminati; a meridie quoque Provincialibus et Apenini devexione clauduntur.

IX

1   Nos autem oportet quam habemus rationem periclitari, cum inquirere intendamus de hiis in quibus nullius autoritate fulcimur, hoc est de unius eiusdemque a principio ydiomatis variatione secuta. Et quia per notiora itinera salubrius breviusque transitur, per illud tantum quod nobis est ydioma pergamus, alia desinentes: nam quod in uno est rationale, videtur in aliis esse causa.

2   Est igitur super quod gradimur ydioma tractando tripharium, ut superius dictum est: nam alii *oc*, alii *sì*, alii vero dicunt *oïl*. Et quod unum fuerit a principio confusionis (quod prius probandum est) apparet, quia convenimus in vocabulis multis, velut eloquentes doctores ostendunt: que quidem convenientia ipsi confusioni repugnat, que ruit celitus in edificatione Babel. Trilingues ergo doctores in multis conveniunt, et

3   maxime in hoc vocabulo quod est 'amor'. Gerardus de Brunel:

> *Si.m sentis fezelz amics,*
> *per ver encusera amor;*

Rex Navarre:

> *De fin amor si vient sen et bonté;*

Dominus Guido Guinizelli:

> *Né fe'amor prima che gentil core,*
> *né gentil ‹cor› prima che amor, natura.*

4   Quare autem tripharie principalius variatum sit, investigemus; et quare quelibet istarum variationum in se ipsa variatur, puta dextre Ytalie locutio ab ea que est sinistre: nam aliter Paduani et aliter Pisani locuntur; et quare vicinius habitantes adhuc discrepant in loquendo, ut Mediolanenses et Veronenses, Romani et Florentini, nec non convenientes in

the same words to signify many things, such as 'God', 'heaven', 'love', 'sea', 'earth', 'is', 'lives', 'dies', 'loves', and almost all others. Of these peoples, those 6 who say *oc* live in the western part of southern Europe, beginning from the boundaries of the Genoese. Those who say *sì*, however, live to the east of those boundaries, all the way to that outcrop of Italy from which the gulf of the Adriatic begins, and in Sicily. But those who say *oïl* live somewhat to the north of these others, for to the east they have the Germans, on the west and north they are hemmed in by the English sea[29] and by the mountains of Aragon, and to the south they are enclosed by the people of Provence and the slopes of the Apennines.

IX

Now I must undertake to risk whatever intelligence I possess, since I 1 intend to enquire into matters in which I can be supported by no authority – that is, into the process of change by which one and the same language became many. And since it is quicker and safer to travel along better-known routes, I shall set out only along that of our own language, leaving the others aside; for what can be seen to be a reason in one case can be assumed to be the cause in others.

The language with which I shall be concerned, then, has three parts, 2 as I said above: for some say *oc*, some say *sì*, and others, indeed, say *oïl*. And the fact – which must first of all be proved[30] – that this language was once unitary, at the time of the primal confusion, is clear, because the three parts agree on so many words, as masters of eloquence and learning show. This agreement denies the very confusion that was hurled down from heaven at the time of the building of Babel. Learned 3 writers in all three vernaculars agree, then, on many words, and especially on the word 'love'. Thus Giraut de Borneil:

Si.m sentis fezelz amics,
per ver encusera amor;[31]

The King of Navarre:

De fin amor si vient sen et bonté;[32]

Master Guido Guinizzelli:

Né fe' amor prima che gentil core,
né gentil ⟨cor⟩ prima che amor, natura.[33]

But now we must investigate why the original[34] language should 4 first have split into three, and why each of the three different forms exhi-

eodem genere gentis, ut Neapolitani et Caetani, Ravennates et Faventini, et, quod mirabilius est, sub eadem civilitate morantes, ut Bononienses
5 Burgi Sancti Felicis et Bononienses Strate Maioris. Hee omnes differentie atque sermonum varietates quid accidant, una eademque ratione patebit.

6 Dicimus ergo quod nullus effectus superat suam causam, in quantum effectus est, quia nil potest efficere quod non est. Cum igitur omnis nostra loquela – preter illam homini primo concreatam a Deo – sit a nostro beneplacito reparata post confusionem illam que nil aliud fuit quam prioris oblivio, et homo sit instabilissimum atque variabilissimum animal, nec durabilis nec continua esse potest, sed sicut alia que nostra sunt, puta mores et habitus, per locorum temporumque distantias
7 variari oportet. Nec dubitandum reor modo in eo quod diximus 'temporum', sed potius opinamur tenendum: nam si alia nostra opera perscrutemur, multo magis discrepare videmur a vetustissimis concivibus nostris quam a coetaneis perlonginquis. Quapropter audacter testamur quod, si vetustissimi Papienses nunc resurgerent, sermone vario vel
8 diverso cum modernis Papiensibus loquerentur. Nec aliter mirum videatur quod dicimus quam percipere iuvenem exoletum quem exolescere non videmus: nam que paulatim moventur, minime perpenduntur a nobis, et quanto longiora tempora variatio rei ad perpendi requirit, tanto
9 rem illam stabiliorem putamus. Non etenim ammiramur si extimationes hominum qui parum distant a brutis putant eandem civitatem sub invariabili semper civicasse sermone, cum sermonis variatio civitatis eiusdem non sine longissima temporum successione paulatim contingat, et
10 hominum vita sit etiam, ipsa sua natura, brevissima. Si ergo per eandem gentem sermo variatur, ut dictum est, successive per tempora, nec stare ullo modo potest, necesse est ut disiunctim abmotimque morantibus varie varietur, ceu varie variantur mores et habitus, qui nec natura nec consortio confirmantur, sed humanis beneplacitis localique congruitate nascuntur.

11 Hinc moti sunt inventores gramatice facultatis: que quidem gramatica nichil aliud est quam quedam inalterabilis locutionis ydemptitas diversibus temporibus atque locis. Hec cum de comuni consensu multarum gentium fuerit regulata, nulli singulari arbitrio videtur obnoxia, et per consequens nec variabilis esse potest. Adinvenerunt ergo illam ne, propter variationem sermonis arbitrio singularium fluitantis, vel nullo modo vel saltim imperfecte antiquorum actingeremus autoritates et gesta, sive illorum quos a nobis locorum diversitas facit esse diversos.

bits variations of its own, so that, for instance, the speech of the right side of Italy differs from that of the left (for the people of Padua speak one way and those of Pisa another).[35] We must also ask why people who live close together still differ in their speech (such as the Milanese and the Veronese, or the Romans and the Florentines); why the same is true of people who originally belonged to the same tribe (such as those of Naples and Gaeta, or Ravenna and Faenza); and, what is still more remarkable, why it is true of people living in the same city (such as the Bolognese of Borgo San Felice and those of Strada Maggiore). It will be clear that all 5 these differences and varieties of speech occur for one and the same reason.

I say, therefore, that no effect exceeds its cause in so far as it is an 6 effect, because nothing can bring about that which it itself is not. Since, therefore, all our language (except that created by God along with the first man) has been assembled, in haphazard fashion, in the aftermath of the great confusion that brought nothing else than oblivion to whatever language had existed before, and since human beings are highly unstable and variable animals, our language can be neither durable nor consistent with itself; but, like everything else that belongs to us (such as manners and customs), it must vary according to distances of space and time. Nor do I think that this principle can be doubted even when I apply 7 it, as I just have, to 'time'; rather, it should be held with conviction. For, if we thoroughly examine other works of humanity, we can see that we differ much more from ancient inhabitants of our own city than from our contemporaries who live far off. On this account, therefore, I make so bold as to declare that if the ancient citizens of Pavia were to rise from the grave, they would speak a language distinct and different from that of the Pavians of today.[36] Nor should what I have just said seem more strange 8 than to see a young man grown to maturity when we have not witnessed his growing. For, when things happen little by little, we scarcely register their progress; and the longer the time that the changes in a thing take to be detected, the more stable we consider that thing to be. Let us not, then, be surprised that, in the opinion of men who differ little from brute 9 beasts, it seems credible that a particular city should always have carried on its affairs in an unchanging language, since changes in a city's speech can only come about gradually, and over a vast span of time; and human life is, by its nature, very short. If, therefore, the speech of a given people 10 changes, as I have said, with the passing of time, and if it can in no way remain stable, it must be the case that the speech of people who live distant and apart from each other also varies in many ways, just as do their manners and customs – which are not maintained either by nature

X

1   Triphario nunc existente nostro ydiomate, ut superius dictum est, in comparatione sui ipsius, secundum quod trisonum factum est, cum tanta timiditate cunctamur librantes quod hanc vel istam vel illam partem in comparando preponere non audemus, nisi eo quo gramatice positores inveniuntur accepisse 'sic' adverbium affirmandi: quod quandam autoritatem erogare videtur Ytalis, qui *sì* dicunt.

2   Quelibet enim partium largo testimonio se tuetur. Allegat ergo pro se lingua *oïl* quod propter sui faciliorem ac delectabiliorem vulgaritatem quicquid redactum est sive inventum ad vulgare prosaycum, suum est: videlicet Biblia cum Troianorum Romanorumque gestibus compilata et Arturi regis ambages pulcerrime et quamplures alie ystorie ac doctrine. Pro se vero argumentatur alia, scilicet *oc*, quod vulgares eloquentes in ea primitus poetati sunt tanquam in perfectiori dulciorique loquela, ut puta Petrus de Alvernia et alii antiquiores doctores. Tertia quoque, ‹que› Latinorum est, se duobus privilegiis actestatur preesse: primo quidem quod qui dulcius subtiliusque poetati vulgariter sunt, hii familiares et domestici sui sunt, puta Cynus Pistoriensis et amicus eius; secundo quia magis videntur initi gramatice que comunis est, quod rationabiliter inspicientibus videtur gravissimum argumentum.

3   Nos vero iudicium relinquentes in hoc et tractatum nostrum ad vulgare latium retrahentes, et receptas in se variationes dicere nec
4   non illas invicem comparare conemur. Dicimus ergo primo Latium bipartitum esse in dextrum et sinistrum. Si quis autem querat de linea dividente, breviter respondemus esse iugum Apenini quod, ceu fistule culmen hinc inde ad diversa stillicidia grundat aquas, ad alterna hinc inde litora per ymbricia longa distillat, ut Lucanus in secundo de-

or association, but arise from people's preferences and geographical proximity.

This was the point from which the inventors of the art of grammar 11 began; for their *gramatica* is nothing less than a certain immutable identity of language in different times and places. Its rules having been formulated with the common consent of many peoples, it can be subject to no individual will; and, as a result, it cannot change. So those who devised this language did so lest, through changes in language dependent on the arbitrary judgement of individuals, we should become either unable, or, at best, only partially able, to enter into contact with the deeds and authoritative writings of the ancients, or of those whose difference of location makes them different from us.

X

Our language now exists in a tripartite form, as I said above; yet, 1 when it comes to assessing its constituent parts on the basis of the three types of sound that they have developed, I find myself timidly hesitating to place any of them in the scale, and not daring to prefer any one to any other for the purposes of comparison, unless it be because those who devised the rules of *gramatica* are known to have chosen the word *sic* as an adverb of affirmation: and this fact would seem to confer a certain pre-eminence on the Italians, who say *sì*.

Indeed each of the three parts could call significant evidence in its 2 own favour. Thus the language of *oïl* adduces on its own behalf the fact that, because of the greater facility and pleasing quality of its vernacular style, everything that is recounted or invented in vernacular prose belongs to it: such as compilations from the Bible and the histories of Troy and Rome,[37] and the beautiful tales of King Arthur,[38] and many other works of history and doctrine. The second part, the language of *oc*, argues in its own favour that eloquent writers in the vernacular first composed poems in this sweeter and more perfect language: they include Peire d'Alvernha and other ancient masters.[39] Finally, the third part, which belongs to the Italians, declares itself to be superior because it enjoys a twofold privilege: first, because those who have written vernacular poetry more sweetly and subtly, such as Cino da Pistoia and his friend, have been its intimates and faithful servants;[40] and second, because they seem to be in the closest contact with the *gramatica* which is shared by all – and this, to those who consider the matter rationally, will appear a very weighty argument.

I will refrain, however, from passing judgement on this question, 3

scribit: dextrum quoque latus Tyrenum mare grundatorium habet,
5 levum vero in Adriaticum cadit. Et dextri regiones sunt Apulia, sed
non tota, Roma, Ducatus, Tuscia et Ianuensis Marchia; sinistri autem
pars Apulie, Marchia Anconitana, Romandiola, Lombardia, Marchia
Trivisiana cum Venetiis. Forum Iulii vero et Ystria non nisi leve Ytalie
esse possunt; nec insule Tyrene maris, videlicet Sicilia et Sardinia, non
6 nisi dextre Ytalie sunt, vel ad dextram Ytaliam sociande. In utroque
quidem duorum laterum, et hiis que secuntur ad ea, lingue hominum
variantur: ut lingua Siculorum cum Apulis, Apulorum cum Romanis,
Romanorum cum Spoletanis, horum cum Tuscis, Tuscorum cum Ia-
nuensibus, Ianuensium cum Sardis; nec non Calabrorum cum Anconi-
tanis, horum cum Romandiolis, Romandiolorum cum Lombardis,
Lombardorum cum Trivisianis et Venetis, horum cum Aquilegiensibus,
et istorum cum Ystrianis. De quo Latinorum neminem nobiscum dis-
sentire putamus.
7   Quare adminus xiiii vulgaribus sola videtur Ytalia variari. Que adhuc
omnia vulgaria in sese variantur, ut puta in Tuscia Senenses et Aretini,
in Lombardia Ferrarenses et Placentini; nec non in eadem civitate ali-
qualem variationem perpendimus, ut superius in capitulo inmediato po-
suimus. Quapropter, si primas et secundarias et subsecundarias vulgaris
Ytalie variationes calculare velimus, et in hoc minimo mundi angulo
non solum ad millenam loquele variationem venire contigerit, sed etiam
ad magis ultra.

and, bringing the discussion back to the Italian vernacular, will try to describe the various forms it has developed, and to compare them one with another. First of all, then, I state that İtaly is divided in two, a 4 left-hand and a right- hand side. If anyone should ask where the dividing-line is drawn, I reply briefly that it is the range of the Apennines; for just as from the topmost rain-gutter[41] water is carried to the ground, dripping down through pipes on each side, these likewise irrigate the whole country through long conduits, on one side and the other, as far as the two opposite shores. All this is described in the second book of Lucan.[42] The drip-tray on the right-hand side is the Tyrrhenian Sea, while the left-hand side drips into the Adriatic. The 5 regions of the right-hand side are Apulia (though not all of it), Rome, the Duchy,[43] Tuscany, and the Genoese Marches; those on the left, however, are the other part of Apulia, the Marches of Ancona, Romagna, Lombardy, the Marches of Treviso, and Venice. As for Friuli and Istria, they can only belong to the left-hand side of Italy, while the islands in the Tyrrhenian – Sicily and Sardinia – clearly belong to the right-hand side, or at least are to be associated with it. On each of the 6 two sides, as well as in the areas associated with them, the language of the inhabitants varies. Thus the language of the Sicilians is different from that of the Apulians, that of the Apulians from that of the Romans, that of the Romans from that of the people of Spoleto, theirs from that of the Tuscans, that of the Tuscans from that of the Genoese, and that of the Genoese from that of the Sardinians; and, likewise, the language of the Calabrians is different from that of the people of Ancona, theirs from that of the people of Romagna, that of the people of Romagna from that of the Lombards, that of the Lombards from that of the people of Treviso and the Venetians, theirs from that of the people of Aquileia, and theirs from that of the Istrians. And I think that no Italian will disagree with me about this.

So we see that Italy alone presents a range of at least fourteen different 7 vernaculars. All these vernaculars also vary internally, so that the Tuscan of Siena is distinguished from that of Arezzo, or the Lombard of Ferrara from that of Piacenza; moreover, we can detect some variation even within a single city, as was suggested above, in the preceding chapter. For this reason, if we wished to calculate the number of primary, and secondary, and still further subordinate varieties of the Italian vernacular, we would find that, even in this tiny corner of the world, the count would take us not only to a thousand different types of speech, but well beyond that figure.

XI

1   Quam multis varietatibus latio dissonante vulgari, decentiorem atque illustremYtalie venemur loquelam; et ut nostre venationi pervium callem habere possimus, perplexos frutices atque sentes prius eiciamus de silva.

2   Sicut ergo Romani se cunctis preponendos existimant, in hac eradicatione sive discerptione non inmerito eos aliis preponamus, protestantes eosdem in nulla vulgaris eloquentie ratione fore tangendos. Dicimus igitur Romanorum non vulgare, sed potius tristiloquium, ytalorum vulgarium omnium esse turpissimum; nec mirum, cum etiam morum habituumque deformitate pre cunctis videantur fetere. Dicunt enim *Messure, quinto dici?*.

3   Post hos incolas Anconitane Marchie decerpamus, qui *Chignamente*
4   *state siate* locuntur: cum quibus et Spoletanos abicimus. Nec pretereundum est quod in improperium istarum trium gentium cantiones quamplures invente sunt: inter quas unam vidimus recte atque perfecte ligatam, quam quidam Florentinus nomine Castra posuerat; incipiebat etenim

Una fermana scopai da Cascioli,
cita cita se 'n gìa 'n grande aina.

5   Post quos Mediolanenses atque Pergameos eorumque finitimos eruncemus, in quorum etiam improperium quendam cecinisse recolimus

Enter l'ora del vesper, ciò fu del mes d'ochiover.

6   Post hos Aquilegienses et Ystrianos cribremus, qui *Ces fas-tu?* crudeliter accentuando eructuant. Cumque hiis montaninas omnes et rusticanas loquelas eicimus, que semper mediastinis civibus accentus enormitate dissonare videntur, ut Casentinenses et Fractenses.

7   Sardos etiam, qui non Latii sunt sed Latiis associandi videntur, eiciamus, quoniam soli sine proprio vulgari esse videntur, gramaticam tanquam simie homines imitantes: nam *domus nova* et *dominus meus* locuntur.

XI

Amid the cacophony of the many varieties of Italian speech, let us 1
hunt for the most respectable and illustrious vernacular that exists in
Italy; and, so that we may have an unobstructed pathway for our
hunting, let us begin by clearing the tangled bushes and brambles out
of the wood.

Accordingly, since the Romans believe that they should always 2
receive preferential treatment, I shall begin this work of pruning or up-
rooting, as is only right, with them; and I do so by declaring that they
should not be taken into account in any didactic work about effective use
of the vernacular. For what the Romans speak is not so much a verna-
cular as a vile jargon, the ugliest of all the languages spoken in Italy; and
this should come as no surprise, for they also stand out among all Italians
for the ugliness of their manners and their outward appearance. They
say things like '*Messure, quinto dici?*'[44]

After these let us prune away the inhabitants of the Marches of 3
Ancona, who say '*Chignamente state siate*';[45] and along with them we
throw out the people of Spoleto. Nor should I fail to mention that a 4
number of poems have been composed in derision of these three peoples;
I have seen one of these, constructed in perfect accordance with the
rules, written by a Florentine of the name of Castra. It began like this:

Una fermana scopai da Cascioli,
cita cita se 'n già 'n grande aina.[46]

After these let us root out the Milanese, the people of Bergamo, and 5
their neighbours; I recall that somebody has written a derisive song
about them too:

Enter l'ora del vesper, ciò fu del mes d'ochiover.[47]

After these let us pass through our sieve the people of Aquileia and 6
Istria, who belch forth '*Ces fas-tu?*'[48] with a brutal intonation. And along
with theirs I reject all languages spoken in the mountains and the coun-
tryside, by people like those of Casentino and Fratta, whose pronounced
accent is always at such odds with that of city-dwellers.

As for the Sardinians, who are not Italian but may be associated with 7
Italians for our purposes, out they must go, because they alone seem to
lack a vernacular of their own, instead imitating *gramatica* as apes do
humans: for they say '*domus nova*' and '*dominus meus*'.[49]

XII

1   Exaceratis quodam modo vulgaribus ytalis, inter ea que remanserunt in cribro comparationem facientes honorabilius atque honorificentius breviter seligamus.

2   Et primo de siciliano examinemus ingenium: nam videtur sicilianum vulgare sibi famam pre aliis asciscere, eo quod quicquid poetantur Ytali sicilianum vocatur, et eo quod perplures doctores indigenas invenimus graviter cecinisse, puta in cantionibus illis

Ancor che l'aigua per lo foco lassi,

et

Amor, che lungiamente m'hai menato.

3   Sed hec fama trinacrie terre, si recte signum ad quod tendit inspiciamus, videtur tantum in obproprium ytalorum principum remansisse, 4   qui non heroico more sed plebeio secuntur superbiam. Siquidem illustres heroes, Fredericus Cesar et benegenitus eius Manfredus, nobilitatem ac rectitudinem sue forme pandentes, donec fortuna permisit, humana secuti sunt, brutalia dedignantes. Propter quod corde nobiles atque gratiarum dotati inherere tantorum principum maiestati conati sunt, ita ut eorum tempore quicquid excellentes animi Latinorum enitebantur primitus in tantorum coronatorum aula prodibat; et quia regale solium erat Sicilia, factum est ut quicquid nostri predecessores vulgariter protulerunt, sicilianum vocetur: quod quidem retinemus et nos, nec posteri nostri permutare valebunt.

5   Racha, racha! Quid nunc personat tuba novissimi Frederici, quid tintinabulum secundi Karoli, quid cornua Iohannis et Azonis marchionum potentum, quid aliorum magnatum tibie, nisi 'Venite carnifices, venite altriplices, venite avaritie sectatores'?

6   Sed prestat ad propositum repedare quam frustra loqui. Et dicimus quod, si vulgare sicilianum accipere volumus secundum quod prodit a terrigenis mediocribus, ex ore quorum iudicium eliciendum videtur, prelationis honore minime dignum est, quia non sine quodam tempore profertur; ut puta ibi:

Tragemi d'este focora se t'este a bolontate.

Si autem ipsum accipere volumus secundum quod ab ore primorum Siculorum emanat, ut in preallegatis cantionibus perpendi potest, nichil differt ab illo quod laudabilissimum est, sicut inferius ostendemus.

XII

Having thus, as best we can, blown away the chaff from among the ver- 1
naculars of Italy, let us compare those that have remained in the sieve
with each other, and quickly make our choice of the one that enjoys and
confers the greatest honour.

First let us turn our attention to the language of Sicily, since the Sici- 2
lian vernacular seems to hold itself in higher regard than any other, first
because all poetry written by Italians is called 'Sicilian', and then because
we do indeed find that many learned natives of that island have written
serious poetry, as, for example, in the *canzoni*

Ancor che l'aigua per lo foco lassi[50]

and

Amor, che lungiamente m'hai menato.[51]

But this fame enjoyed by the Trinacrian isle,[52] if we carefully consider 3
the end to which it leads, seems rather to survive only as a reproof to the
princes of Italy, who are so puffed up with pride that they live in a ple-
beian, not a heroic, fashion. Indeed, those illustrious heroes, the 4
Emperor Frederick and his worthy son Manfred, knew how to reveal the
nobility and integrity that were in their hearts; and, as long as fortune
allowed, they lived in a manner befitting men, despising the bestial life.[53]
On this account, all who were noble of heart and rich in graces[54] strove
to attach themselves to the majesty of such worthy princes, so that, in
their day, all that the most gifted individuals in Italy brought forth first
came to light in the court of these two great monarchs. And since Sicily
was the seat of the imperial throne, it came about that whatever our pre-
decessors wrote in the vernacular was called 'Sicilian'. This term is still in
use today, and posterity will be able to do nothing to change it.[55]

Racha, racha![56] What is the noise made now by the trumpet of the 5
latest Frederick, or the bells of the second Charles, or the horns of the
powerful marquises Giovanni and Azzo, or the pipes of the other war-
lords?[57] Only 'Come, you butchers! Come, you traitors! Come, you devo-
tees of greed!'

But I should rather return to my subject than waste words like this. 6
So I say that, if by Sicilian vernacular we mean what is spoken by the
average inhabitants of the island – and they should clearly be our stan-
dard of comparison – then this is far from worthy of the honour of
heading the list, because it cannot be pronounced without a certain
drawl, as in this case:

7   Apuli quoque vel sui acerbitate vel finitimorum suorum contiguitate, qui Romani et Marchiani sunt, turpiter barbarizant: dicunt enim

Bòlzera che chiangesse lo quatraro.

8   Sed quamvis terrigene Apuli loquantur obscene comuniter, prefulgentes eorum quidam polite locuti sunt, vocabula curialiora in suis cantionibus compilantes, ut manifeste apparet eorum dicta perspicientibus, ut puta

Madonna, dir vi voglio,

et

Per fino amore vo sì letamente.

9   Quapropter superiora notantibus innotescere debet nec siculum nec apulum esse illud quod in Ytalia pulcerrimum est vulgare, cum eloquentes indigenas ostenderimus a proprio divertisse.

XIII

1   Post hec veniamus ad Tuscos, qui propter amentiam suam infroniti titulum sibi vulgaris illustris arrogare videntur. Et in hoc non solum plebeia dementat intentio, sed famosos quamplures viros hoc tenuisse comperimus: puta Guittonem Aretinum, qui nunquam se ad curiale vulgare direxit, Bonagiuntam Lucensem, Gallum Pisanum, Minum Mocatum Senensem, Brunectum Florentinum: quorum dicta, si rimari vacaverit, non curialia sed municipalia tantum invenientur.

2   Et quoniam Tusci pre aliis in hac ebrietate baccantur, dignum utileque videtur municipalia vulgaria Tuscanorum sigillatim in aliquo depompare. Locuntur Florentini et dicunt *Manichiamo, introcque che noi non facciamo altro.* Pisani: *Bene andonno li fatti de Fiorensa per Pisa.* Lucenses: *Fo voto a Dio ke in grassarra eie lo comuno de Lucca.* Senenses: *Onche renegata*

3   *avess'io Siena. Ch'ee* chesto? Aretini: *Vuo' tu venire ovelle?* De Perusio, Urbe Veteri, Viterbio, nec non de Civitate Castellana, propter affinitatem quam

Tragemi d'este focora se t'este a bolontate.[58]

If, however, we mean what emerges from the mouths of the leading citizens of Sicily – examples of which may be found in the *canzoni* quoted above – then it is in no way distinguishable from the most praiseworthy variety of the vernacular, as I shall show below.

The people of Apulia, to continue, whether through their own native 7 crudity or through the proximity of their neighbours (the Romans and the people of the Marches), use many gross barbarisms: they say

Bòlzera che chiangesse lo quatraro.[59]

But although the inhabitants of Apulia generally speak in a base 8 fashion, some of the most distinguished among them have managed to attain a more refined manner, by including courtlier words in their poetry. This will be clear to anyone who examines their works, such as

Madonna, dir vi voglio,[60]

and

Per fino amore vo sì letamente.[61]

Therefore, if we take due account of what was said above, it seems irre- 9 futable that neither Sicilian nor the language of Apulia can be the most beautiful of the Italian vernaculars, since, as I have shown, the most eloquent natives of the two regions have preferred not to use them.

XIII

After this, we come to the Tuscans, who, rendered senseless by some 1 aberration of their own, seem to lay claim to the honour of possessing the illustrious vernacular. And it is not only the common people who lose their heads in this fashion, for we find that a number of famous men have believed as much: like Guittone d'Arezzo,[62] who never even aimed at a vernacular worthy of the court, or Bonagiunta da Lucca,[63] or Gallo of Pisa,[64] or Mino Mocato of Siena,[65] or Brunetto the Florentine,[66] all of whose poetry, if there were space to study it closely here, we would find to be fitted not for a court but at best for a city council.

Now, since the Tuscans are the most notorious victims of this mental 2 intoxication, it seems both appropriate and useful to examine the vernaculars of the cities of Tuscany one by one, and thus to burst the bubble of their pride. When the Florentines speak, they say things like: '*Manichiamo, introcque che noi non facciamo altro.*'[67] The Pisans: '*Bene andonno li*

4 habent cum Romanis et Spoletanis, nichil tractare intendimus. Sed
quanquam fere omnes Tusci in suo turpiloquio sint obtusi, nonnullos
vulgaris excellentiam cognovisse sentimus, scilicet Guidonem, Lapum
et unum alium, Florentinos, et Cynum Pistoriensem, quem nunc indigne
5 postponimus, non indigne coacti. Itaque si tuscanas examinemus lo-
quelas, et pensemus qualiter viri prehonorati a propria diverterunt, non
restat in dubio quin aliud sit vulgare quod querimus quam quod actingit
populus Tuscanorum.
6 Si quis autem quod de Tuscis asserimus, de Ianuensibus asserendum
non putet, hoc solum in mente premat, quod si per oblivionem Ianuenses
ammicterent z licteram, vel mutire totaliter eos vel novam reparare opor-
teret loquelam. Est enim z maxima pars eorum locutionis: que quidem
lictera non sine multa rigiditate profertur.

XIV

1 Transeuntes nunc humeros Apenini frondiferos levam Ytaliam con-
tatim venemur ceu solemus, orientaliter ineuntes.
2 Romandiolam igitur ingredientes, dicimus nos duo in Latio invenisse
vulgaria quibusdam convenientiis contrariis alternata. Quorum unum
in tantum muliebre videtur propter vocabulorum et prolationis molli-
tiem quod virum, etiam si viriliter sonet, feminam tamen facit esse cre-
3 dendum. Hoc Romandiolos omnes habet, et presertim Forlivienses,
quorum civitas, licet novissima sit, meditullium tamen esse videtur
totius provincie: hii *deusci* affirmando locuntur, et *oclo meo* et *corada mea*
proferunt blandientes. Horum aliquos a proprio poetando divertisse
4 audivimus, Thomam videlicet et Ugolinum Bucciolam, Faventinos. Est et
aliud, sicut dictum est, adeo vocabulis accentibusque yrsutum et
yspidum quod propter sui rudem asperitatem mulierem loquentem non
5 solum disterminat, sed esse virum dubitares, lector. Hoc omnes qui
magara dicunt, Brixianos videlicet, Veronenses et Vigentinos, habet; nec
non Paduanos, turpiter sincopantes omnia in '–tus' participia et denomi-
nativa in '–tas', ut *mercò* et *bontè*. Cum quibus et Trivisianos adducimus,

fatti de Fiorensa per Pisa.[68] The people of Lucca: *'Fo voto a Dio ke in grassarra eie lo comuno de Lucca.'*[69] The Sienese: *'Onche reŋegata avess'io Siena. Ch'ee chesto?'*[70] The people of Arezzo: *'Vuo' tu venire ovelle?'*[71] I have no inten- 3 tion of dealing with Perugia, Orvieto, Viterbo, or Città di Castello, because of their inhabitants' affinity with the Romans and the people of Spoleto. However, though almost all Tuscans are steeped in their own foul jargon, 4 there are a few, I feel, who have understood the excellence of the vernacular: these include Guido, Lapo, and one other, all from Florence, and Cino, from Pistoia, whom I place unworthily here at the end, moved by a consideration that is far from unworthy.[72] Therefore, if we study the lan- 5 guages spoken in Tuscany, and if we think what kind of distinguished individuals have avoided the use of their own, there can be no doubt that the vernacular we seek is something other than that which the people of Tuscany can attain.

If there is anyone who thinks that what I have just said about the 6 Tuscans could not be applied to the Genoese, let him consider only that if, through forgetfulness, the people of Genoa lost the use of the letter *z*, they would either have to fall silent for ever or invent a new language for themselves. For *z* forms the greater part of their vernacular, and it is, of course, a letter that cannot be pronounced without considerable harshness.

XIV

Let us now traverse the leafy shoulders of the Apennines, and con- 1 tinue our hunt, in the accustomed manner, on the left-hand side of Italy, beginning from the east.

Our first encounter, therefore, is with the language of Romagna, of 2 which I say that in this part of Italy are found two vernaculars which stand in direct opposition to each other because of certain contradictory features. One of them is so womanish, because of the softness of its vocabulary and pronunciation, that a man who speaks it, even if in a suitably virile manner, still ends up being mistaken for a woman. This is spoken by 3 everybody in Romagna, especially the people of Forlì, whose city, despite being near the edge of the region, none the less seems to be the focal point of the whole province: they say *'deuscì'*[73] when they wish to say 'yes', and to seduce someone they say *'oclo meo'*[74] and *'corada med'.*[75] I have heard that some of them depart from their native speech in their poetry; these include Tommaso, and Ugolino Bucciòla, both of Faenza.[76] There is also 4 another vernacular, as I said, so hirsute and shaggy in its vocabulary and accent that, because of its brutal harshness, it not only destroys the femi-

qui more Brixianorum et finitimorum suorum *u* consonantem per *f* apoc-
opando proferunt, puta *nof* pro 'novem' et *vif* pro 'vivo': quod quidem bar-
barissimum reprobamus.

6   Veneti quoque nec sese investigati vulgaris honore dignantur; et si
quis eorum, errore confossus, vanitaret in hoc, recordetur si unquam
dixit

Per le plaghe di Dio tu no verras.

7   Inter quos omnes unum audivimus nitentem divertere a materno et
ad curiale vulgare intendere, videlicet Ildebrandinum Paduanum.

8   Quare, omnibus presentis capituli ad iudicium comparentibus, arbi-
tramur nec romandiolum nec suum oppositum, ut dictum est, nec vene-
tianum esse illud quod querimus vulgare illustre.

XV

1   Illud autem quod de ytalia silva residet percontari conemur expe-
dientes.

2   Dicimus ergo quod forte non male opinantur qui Bononienses as-
serunt pulcriori locutione loquentes, cum ab Ymolensibus, Ferrarensibus
et Mutinensibus circunstantibus aliquid proprio vulgari asciscunt, sicut
facere quoslibet a finitimis suis conicimus, ut Sordellus de Mantua sua
ostendit, Cremone, Brixie atque Verone confini: qui, tantus eloquentie vir
existens, non solum in poetando sed quomodocunque loquendo patrium
3   vulgare deseruit. Accipiunt enim prefati cives ab Ymolensibus lenitatem
atque mollitiem, a Ferrarensibus vero et Mutinensibus aliqualem garru-
litatem que proprie Lombardorum est: hanc ex commixtione advenarum
4   Longobardorum terrigenis credimus remansisse. Et hec est causa quare
Ferrarensium, Mutinensium vel Regianorum nullum invenimus poe-
tasse: nam proprie garrulitati assuefacti nullo modo possunt ad vulgare
aulicum sine quadam acerbitate venire. Quod multo magis de Parmen-
sibus est putandum, qui *monto* pro 'multo' dicunt.

ninity of any woman who speaks it, but, reader, would make you think 5
her a man. This is the speech of all those who say '*magara*',[77] such as the citizens of Brescia, Verona and Vicenza; and the Paduans also speak like this, when they cruelly cut short all the participles ending in *tus* and the nouns in *tas*, saying '*mercò*' [78] and '*bontè*'.[79] Along with these I will mention the people of Treviso, who, like those of Brescia and their neighbours, abbreviate their words by pronouncing consonantal *u* as *f*, saying '*nof*' for '*nove*' [80] and '*vif*' for '*vivo*'.[81] This I denounce as the height of barbarism.

Nor can the Venetians be considered worthy of the honour due to the 6 vernacular for which we are searching; and if any of them, transfixed by error, be tempted to take pride in his speech, let him remember if he ever said

Per le plaghe di Dio tu no verras.[82]

Among all these peoples I have heard only one individual who tried 7 to break free of his mother-tongue and aspire to a vernacular worthy of the court, and that was Aldobrandino Padovano.[83]

So on all the vernaculars that have presented themselves before the 8 tribunal of the present chapter I pronounce the following verdict: that neither the language of Romagna, nor its opposite described above, nor Venetian is that illustrious vernacular which we are seeking.

XV

I shall now try to bring to a rapid conclusion our hunt through what 1 remains of the Italian forest.

I say, then, that perhaps those are not wrong who claim that the Bolog- 2 nese speak a more beautiful language than most, especially since they take many features of their own speech from that of the people who live around them, in Imola, Ferrara and Modena. I believe that everybody does this with respect to his own neighbours, as is shown by the case of Sordello of Mantua, on the borders of Cremona, Brescia, and Verona: this man of unusual eloquence abandoned the vernacular of his home town not only when writing poetry but on every other occasion.[84] So the 3 above-mentioned citizens of Bologna take a soft, yielding quality from those of Imola, and from the people of Ferrara and Modena, on the other hand, a certain abruptness which is more typical of the Lombards (to whom it was left, I believe, after the mingling of the original inhabitants of the area with the invading Longobards). And this is why we find that 4 no one from Ferrara, Modena, or Reggio has written poetry; for, being ac-

5   Si ergo Bononienses utrinque accipiunt, ut dictum est, rationabile videtur esse quod eorum locutio per commixtionem oppositorum ut dictum est ad laudabilem suavitatem remaneat temperata: quod procul
6   dubio nostro iudicio sic esse censemus. Itaque si preponentes eos in vulgari sermone sola municipalia Latinorum vulgaria comparando considerant, allubescentes concordamus cum illis; si vero simpliciter vulgare bononiense preferendum existimant, dissentientes discordamus ab eis. Non etenim est quod aulicum et illustre vocamus: quoniam, si fuisset, maximus Guido Guinizelli, Guido Ghisilerius, Fabrutius et Honestus et alii poetantes Bononie nunquam a proprio divertissent: qui doctores fuerunt illustres et vulgarium discretione repleti. Maximus Guido:

Madonna,'l fino amore ch'io vi porto;

Guido Ghisilerius:

Donna, lo fermo core;

Fabrutius:

Lo meo lontano gire;

Honestus:

Più non attendo il tuo soccorso, amore.

Que quidem verba prorsus a mediastinis Bononie sunt diversa.

7   Cumque de residuis in extremis Ytalie civitatibus neminem dubitare pendamus – et si quis dubitat, illum nulla nostra solutione dignamur –, parum restat in nostra discussione dicendum. Quare, cribellum cupientes deponere, ut residentiam cito visamus, dicimus Tridentum atque Taurinum nec non Alexandriam civitates metis Ytalie in tantum sedere propinquas quod puras nequeunt habere loquelas; ita quod, si etiam quod turpissimum habent vulgare, haberent pulcerrimum, propter aliorum commixtionem esse vere latium negaremus. Quare, si latium illustre venamur, quod venamur in illis inveniri non potest.

customed to their native abruptness, they could not approach the high poetic vernacular without betraying a certain lack of sophistication. And the same must also be thought, with still greater conviction, of the people of Parma, who say '*monto*' when they mean '*molto*'.[85]

If, then, the Bolognese take from all sides, as I have said, it seems rea- 5 sonable to suggest that their language, tempered by the combination of opposites mentioned above, should achieve a praiseworthy degree of elegance; and this, in my opinion, is beyond doubt true. Therefore, if theirs is 6 put forward as the most admirable of vernaculars on the basis of a comparison of all the languages actually spoken in the different cities of Italy, I will agree wholeheartedly; if, however, it were to be suggested that the Bolognese vernacular should be given pride of place in absolute terms, then, dissenting, I must register my firm disagreement. For it is not what we could call 'aulic' or 'illustrious' language; if it were, Bolognese poets like the great Guido Guinizzelli, or Guido Ghislieri, or Fabruzzo or Onesto or many others, would never have left off using it.[86] Yet these were distinguished men of learning, who fully understood the nature of the vernacular. The great Guido wrote

Madonna, 'l fino amore ch'io vi porto;[87]

Guido Ghislieri:

Donna, lo fermo core;[88]

Fabruzzo:

Lo meo lontano gire;[89]

Onesto:

Più non attendo il tuo soccorso, amore.[90]

All these words are very different from what you will hear in the heart of Bologna.

As for the remaining cities located on the furthest edges of Italy, I do 7 not think that anyone can have doubts about them – and if he has, I will waste no explanations on him. So there remains little to be said about our present subject. On which account, and in order to survey quickly what is left (for I am anxious to lay down my sieve), I say that Trento and Turin, in my opinion, along with Alessandria, are situated so close to the boundaries of Italy that they could not possibly speak a pure language. So, even if they possessed the most beautiful of vernaculars – and the ones they do have are appalling – I would deny that their speech is truly Italian, because of its contamination by that of others. I conclude, therefore, that

XVI

1   Postquam venati saltus et pascua sumus Ytalie, nec pantheram quam sequimur adinvenimus, ut ipsam reperire possimus rationabilius investigemus de illa ut, solerti studio, redolentem ubique et necubi apparentem nostris penitus irretiamus tenticulis.

2   Resumentes igitur venabula nostra, dicimus quod in omni genere rerum unum esse oportet quo generis illius omnia comparentur et ponderentur, et a quo omnium aliorum mensuram accipiamus: sicut in numero cuncta mensurantur uno, et plura vel pauciora dicuntur secundum quod distant ab uno vel ei propinquant, et sicut in coloribus omnes albo mensurantur – nam visibiles magis et minus dicuntur secundum quod accedunt vel recedunt ab albo. Et quemadmodum de hiis dicimus que quantitatem et qualitatem ostendunt, de predicamentorum quolibet, etiam de substantia, posse dici putamus: scilicet ut unumquodque mensurabile sit, secundum quod in genere est, illo quod simpli-

3   cissimum est in ipso genere. Quapropter in actionibus nostris, quantumcunque dividantur in species, hoc signum inveniri oportet quo et ipse mensurentur. Nam, in quantum simpliciter ut homines agimus, virtutem habemus – ut generaliter illam intelligamus –: nam secundum ipsam bonum et malum hominem iudicamus; in quantum ut homines cives agimus, habemus legem, secundum quam dicitur civis bonus et malus; in quantum ut homines latini agimus, quedam habemus simplicissima signa et morum et habituum et locutionis, quibus latine actiones

4   ponderantur et mensurantur. Que quidem nobilissima sunt earum que Latinorum sunt actiones, hec nullius civitatis Ytalie propria sunt, et in omnibus comunia sunt: inter que nunc potest illud discerni vulgare quod superius venabamur, quod in qualibet redolet civitate nec cubat in

5   ulla. Potest tamen magis in una quam in alia redolere, sicut simplicissima substantiarum, que Deus est, in homine magis redolet quam in bruto, in animali quam in planta, in hac quam in minera, in hac quam in elemento, in igne quam in terra; et simplicissima quantitas, quod est unum, in impari numero redolet magis quam in pari; et simplicissimus color, qui albus est, magis in citrino quam in viride redolet.

6   Itaque, adepti quod querebamus, dicimus illustre, cardinale, aulicum et curiale vulgare in Latio, quod omnis latie civitatis est et nullius esse videtur, et quo municipalia vulgaria omnia Latinorum mensurantur et ponderantur et comparantur.

if we are hunting an illustrious form of Italian, our prey is not to be found in any of these cities.

XVI

Now that we have hunted across the woodlands and pastures of all 1 Italy without finding the panther we are trailing, let us, in the hope of tracking it down, carry out a more closely reasoned investigation, so that, by the assiduous practice of cunning, we can at last entice into our trap this creature whose scent is left everywhere but which is nowhere to be seen. .

Accordingly, I take up my equipment once more for the hunt, and 2 state that in any kind of thing there needs to be one instance with which all others can be compared, against which they can be weighed, and from which we derive the standard by which all others are measured.[91] Thus, in arithmetic, all numbers are measured by comparison with the number one, and are deemed larger or smaller according to their relative distance from or closeness to that number. Likewise with colours, all are measured against white, and held to be brighter or darker as they approach or recede from that colour. And I hold that what can be said of things that have quantity and quality is also true of any predicate whatever, and even of substances: in short, that everything can be measured, in so far as it belongs to a genus, by comparison with the simplest individual found in that genus. Therefore, when dealing with human actions, 3 in so far as these can be allotted to different categories, we must be able to define a standard against which these too can be measured. Now, in so far as we act simply as human beings, we possess a capacity to act – a 'virtue', if we understand this in a general sense – and according to this we judge people to be good or bad. In so far as we act as human beings who are citizens, we have the law, by whose standards we can describe a citizen as good or bad; in so far as we act as human beings who are Italians, there are certain very simple features, of manners and appearance and speech, by which the actions of the people of Italy can be weighed and measured. But the most noble actions among those performed by Ita- 4 lians are proper to no one Italian city, but are common to them all; and among these we can now place the use of the vernacular that we were hunting above, which has left its scent in every city but made its home in none. Its scent may still be stronger in one city than another, just as the 5 simplest of substances, which is God, is more clearly present in human beings than in animals, in animals than in plants,[92] in plants than in minerals, in minerals than in the basic element, and in fire than in earth;

XVII

1   Quare autem hoc quod repertum est, illustre, cardinale, aulicum et curiale adicientes vocemus, nunc disponendum est: per quod clarius ipsum quod ipsum est faciamus patere.

2   Primum igitur quid intendimus cum illustre adicimus, et quare illustre dicimus, denudemus. Per hoc quoque quod illustre dicimus, intelligimus quid illuminans et illuminatum prefulgens: et hoc modo viros appellamus illustres, vel quia potestate illuminati alios et iustitia et karitate illuminant, vel quia excellenter magistrati excellenter magistrent, ut Seneca et Numa Pompilius. Et vulgare de quo loquimur et sublimatum est magistratu et potestate, et suos honore sublimat et gloria.

3   Magistratu quidem sublimatum videtur, cum de tot rudibus Latinorum vocabulis, de tot perplexis constructionibus, de tot defectivis prolationibus, de tot rusticanis accentibus, tam egregium, tam extricatum, tam perfectum et tam urbanum videamus electum ut Cynus Pistoriensis et amicus eius ostendunt in cantionibus suis.

4   Quod autem exaltatum sit potestate, videtur. Et quid maioris potestatis est quam quod humana corda versare potest, ita ut nolentem volentem et volentem nolentem faciat, velut ipsum et fecit et facit?

5   Quod autem honore sublimet, in promptu est. Nonne domestici sui
6   reges, marchiones, comites et magnates quoslibet fama vincunt? Minime hoc probatione indiget. Quantum vero suos familiares gloriosos efficiat, nos ipsi novimus, qui huius dulcedine glorie nostrum exilium postergamus.

7   Quare ipsum illustre merito profiteri debemus.

or as the simplest quantity, one, is more apparent in odd numbers than in even; or as the simplest colour, white, shines more visibly in yellow than in green.

So we have found what we were seeking: we can define the illustrious,   6
cardinal, aulic, and curial vernacular in Italy as that which belongs to every Italian city yet seems to belong to none, and against which the vernaculars of all the cities of the Italians can be measured, weighed, and compared.

XVII

Now, however, it becomes necessary to explain why what we have   1
found should be given the epithets 'illustrious', 'cardinal', 'aulic', and 'curial'; and by so doing I shall reveal more clearly what the phenomenon is in itself.

First of all, therefore, I shall explain what I mean when I use the term   2
'illustrious', and why it is applied to the vernacular. Now when we call something 'illustrious', we mean that it gives off light or reflects the light that it receives from elsewhere: and we call men 'illustrious' in this sense, either because, enlightened by power, they shine forth justice and charity upon other people, or because, excellently taught, they teach most excellently, like Seneca or Numa Pompilius.[93] And this vernacular of which I speak is both sublime in learning and power, and capable of exalting those who use it in honour and glory.

That it is sublime in learning is clear when we see it emerge, so out-   3
standing, so lucid, so perfect and so civilised, from among so many ugly words used by Italians, so many convoluted constructions, so many defective formations, and so many barbarous pronunciations – as Cino da Pistoia and his friend show us in their *canzoni*.

That it is exalted in power is plain. And what greater power could   4
there be than that which can melt the hearts of human beings, so as to make the unwilling willing and the willing unwilling, as it has done and still does?

That it raises to honour is readily apparent. Does not the fame of its de-   5
votees exceed that of any king, marquis, count or warlord? There is no   6
need to prove this. And I myself have known how greatly it increases the glory of those who serve it, I who, for the sake of that glory's sweetness, have the experience of exile behind me.

For all these reasons we are right to call this vernacular 'illustrious'.   7

XVIII

1 Neque sine ratione ipsum vulgare illustre decusamus adiectione secunda, videlicet ut id cardinale vocetur. Nam sicut totum hostium cardinem sequitur ut, quo cardo vertitur, versetur et ipsum, seu introrsum seu extrorsum flectatur, sic et universus municipalium grex vulgarium vertitur et revertitur, movetur et pausat secundum quod istud, quod quidem vere paterfamilias esse videtur. Nonne cotidie extirpat sentosos frutices de ytalia silva? Nonne cotidie vel plantas inserit vel plantaria plantat? Quid aliud agricole sui satagunt nisi ut amoveant et admoveant, ut dictum est? Quare prorsus tanto decusari vocabulo promeretur.

2 Quia vero aulicum nominamus illud causa est quod, si aulam nos Ytali haberemus, palatinum foret. Nam si aula totius regni comunis est domus et omnium regni partium gubernatrix augusta, quicquid tale est ut omnibus sit comune nec proprium ulli, conveniens est ut in ea conversetur et habitet, nec aliquod aliud habitaculum tanto dignum est habi-

3 tante: hoc nempe videtur esse id de quo loquimur vulgare. Et hinc est quod in regiis omnibus conversantes semper illustri vulgari locuntur; hinc etiam est quod nostrum illustre velut acola peregrinatur et in humilibus hospitatur asilis, cum aula vacemus.

4 Est etiam merito curiale dicendum, quia curialitas nil aliud est quam librata regula eorum que peragenda sunt: et quia statera huiusmodi librationis tantum in excellentissimis curiis esse solet, hinc est quod quicquid in actibus nostris bene libratum est, curiale dicatur. Unde cum istud in excellentissima Ytalorum curia sit libratum, dici curiale meretur.

5 Sed dicere quod in excellentissima Ytalorum curia sit libratum, videtur nugatio, cum curia careamus. Ad quod facile respondetur: nam licet curia, secundum quod unita accipitur, ut curia regis Alamannie, in Ytalia non sit, membra tamen eius non desunt; et sicut membra illius uno Principe uniuntur, sic membra huius gratioso lumine rationis unita sunt. Quare falsum esset dicere curia carere Ytalos, quanquam Principe careamus, quoniam curiam habemus, licet corporaliter sit dispersa.

XVIII

Nor are we without justification if we adorn this illustrious vernacular 1
with our second epithet, by calling it 'cardinal'.[94] For, just as the whole
structure of a door obeys its hinge, so that in whatever direction the
hinge moves, the door moves with it, whether it opens towards the inside
or the outside, so the whole flock of languages spoken in the cities of Italy
turns this way or that, moves or stands still, at the behest of this verna-
cular, which thus shows itself to be the true head of their family. Does it
not daily dig up thorn-bushes growing in the Italian forest? Does it not
daily make new grafts or prick out seedlings? What else do its gardeners
do, if they are not uprooting or planting, as I said earlier? For this reason it
has fully earned the right to deck itself out with so noble an epithet.

The reason for calling this vernacular 'aulic', on the other hand, is 2
that if we Italians had a royal court, it would make its home in the court's
palace. For if the court is the shared home of the entire kingdom, and the
honoured governor of every part of it, it is fitting that everything that is
common to all yet owned by none should frequent the court and live
there; and indeed no other dwelling-place would be worthy of such a resi-
dent. And this certainly seems to be true of this vernacular of which I 3
speak. So this is why those who frequent any royal court always speak an
illustrious vernacular; it is also why our illustrious vernacular wanders
around like a homeless stranger, finding hospitality in more humble
homes – because we have no court.

It is right to call this vernacular 'curial', because the essence of being 4
curial is no more than providing a balanced assessment of whatever has
to be dealt with; and because the scales on which this assessment is
carried out are usually found only in the most authoritative of tribunals,
whatever is well balanced in our actions is called 'curial'. Therefore, since
this vernacular has been assessed before the most excellent tribunal in
Italy, it deserves to be called 'curial'.[95]

Yet it seems contradictory to say that it has been assessed in the most 5
excellent tribunal in Italy, since we have no such tribunal. The answer to
this is simple. For although it is true that there is no such tribunal in Italy
– in the sense of a single institution, like that of the king of Germany[96] –
yet its constituent elements are not lacking. And just as the elements of
the German tribunal are united under a single monarch, so those of the
Italian have been brought together by the gracious light of reason. So it
would not be true to say that the Italians lack a tribunal altogether, even
though we lack a monarch, because we do have one, but its physical com-
ponents are scattered.

XIX

1   Hoc autem vulgare quod illustre, cardinale, aulicum et curiale os-
tensum est, dicimus esse illud quod vulgare latium appellatur. Nam sicut
quoddam vulgare est invenire quod proprium est Cremone, sic quoddam
est invenire quod proprium est Lombardie; et sicut est invenire aliquod
quod sit proprium Lombardie, ‹sic› est invenire aliquod quod sit totius si-
nistre Ytalie proprium; et sicut omnia hec est invenire, sic et illud quod
totius Ytalie est. Et sicut illud cremonense ac illud lombardum et tertium
semilatium dicitur, sic istud, quod totius Ytalie est, latium vulgare
vocatur. Hoc enim usi sunt doctores illustres qui lingua vulgari poetati
sunt in Ytalia, ut Siculi, Apuli, Tusci, Romandioli, Lombardi et utriusque
Marchie viri.

2   Et quia intentio nostra, ut polliciti sumus in principio huius operis,
est doctrinam de vulgari eloquentia tradere, ab ipso tanquam ab excel-
lentissimo incipientes, quos putamus ipso dignos uti, et propter quid, et
quomodo, nec non ubi, et quando, et ad quos ipsum dirigendum sit, in in-
3   mediatis libris tractabimus. Quibus illuminatis, inferiora vulgaria illumi-
nare curabimus, gradatim descendentes ad illud quod unius solius
familie proprium est.

XIX

So now we can say that this vernacular, which has been shown to be il- 1
lustrious, cardinal, aulic, and[97] curial, is the vernacular that is called
Italian. For, just as one vernacular can be identified as belonging to
Cremona, so can another that belongs to Lombardy; and just as one can
be identified that belongs to Lombardy, so can another that belongs to the
whole left-hand side of Italy; and just as all these can be identified in this
way, so can that which belongs to Italy as a whole. And just as the first is
called Cremonese, the second Lombard, and the third half-Italian, so this
last, which belongs to all Italy, is called the Italian vernacular. This is the
language used by the illustrious authors who have written vernacular
poetry in Italy, whether they came from Sicily, Apulia, Tuscany,
Romagna, Lombardy, or either of the Marches.

And since my intention, as I promised at the beginning of this work, 2
is to teach a theory of the effective use of the vernacular, I have begun
with this form of it, as being the most excellent; and I shall go on, in the
following books,[98] to discuss the following questions: whom I think
worthy of using this language, for what purpose, in what manner, where,
when, and what audience they should address. Having clarified all this, I 3
shall attempt to throw some light on the question of the less important
vernaculars, descending step by step until I reach the language that
belongs to a single family.

Liber Secundus

I

1 Sollicitantes iterum celeritatem ingenii nostri et ad calamum frugi operis redeuntes, ante omnia confitemur latium vulgare illustre tam prosayce quam metrice decere proferri. Sed quia ipsum prosaycantes ab avientibus magis accipiunt et quia quod avietum est prosaycantibus permanere videtur exemplar, et non e converso – que quendam videntur prebere primatum –, primo secundum quod metricum est ipsum carminemus, ordine pertractantes illo quem in fine primi libri polluximus.

2 Queramus igitur prius utrum omnes versificantes vulgariter debeant illud uti. Et superficietenus videtur quod sic, quia omnis qui versificatur suos versus exornare debet in quantum potest: quare, cum nullum sit tam grandis exornationis quam vulgare illustre, videtur quod

3 quisquis versificator debeat ipsum uti. Preterea, quod optimum est in genere suo, si suis inferioribus misceatur, non solum nil derogare videtur eis, sed ea meliorare videtur: quare si quis versificator, quanquam rude versificetur, ipsum sue ruditati admisceat, non solum bene facit, sed ipsum sic facere oportere videtur: multo magis opus est adiutorio illis qui pauca quam qui multa possunt. Et sic apparet quod omnibus versificantibus liceat ipsum uti.

4 Sed hoc falsissimum est: quia nec semper excellentissime poetantes debent illud induere, sicut per inferius pertractata perpendi poterit.

5 Exigit ergo istud sibi consimiles viros, quemadmodum alii nostri mores et habitus – exigit enim magnificentia magna potentes, purpura viros nobiles: sic et hoc excellentes ingenio et scientia querit, et alios asper-

6 natur, ut per inferiora patebit. Nam quicquid nobis convenit, vel gratia generis, vel speciei, vel individui convenit, ut sentire, ridere, militare. Sed hoc non convenit nobis gratia generis, quia etiam brutis conveniret; nec gratia speciei, quia cunctis hominibus esset conveniens, de quo nulla questio est – nemo enim montaninis rusticana tractantibus hoc dicet

7 esse conveniens –: convenit ergo individui gratia. Sed nichil individuo convenit nisi per proprias dignitates, puta mercari, militare ac regere: quare si convenientia respiciunt dignitates, hoc est dignos, et quidam

46

Book Two

I

Once more I call upon the resources of my swift-moving intellect, 1
take up once more the pen used in my fruitful labours, and first of all
declare that the illustrious Italian vernacular may as fittingly be used for
writing prose as for writing poetry. But, because writers of prose most
often learn the vernacular from poets,[99] and because what is set out in
poetry serves as a model for those who write prose, and not the other way
about – which would seem to confer a certain primacy – I shall first
expound the principles[100] according to which the illustrious vernacular
is used for writing poetry, following the order of treatment laid down at
the end of the first book.

Let us first ask, then, whether all who write poetry in the vernacular 2
should use it in its illustrious form. To a superficial enquirer it might seem
that they should, because anyone who writes poetry should embellish
his lines as much as possible; and therefore, since nothing provides as
splendid an ornament as does the illustrious vernacular, it seems that
any writer of poetry should use it. Moreover, anything that is the best of 3
its kind, if it be mixed with what is inferior to it, not only takes nothing
away from the lesser material, but actually improves it; and therefore if
poets, however crude the verses they write, mix the illustrious verna-
cular with their own crudities, they not only do the right thing but, it
seems, are obliged to do so: those of limited ability stand much more in
need of help than those with greater skill. And so it seems obvious that all
poets have the right to use the illustrious vernacular.

Yet this is completely untrue, because not even the best of poets 4
should use it on every occasion, as will be made clear by the thorough dis-
cussion below. The illustrious vernacular requires, in fact, that those 5
who use it have true affinity with it, as is the case with our other customs
and symbols of authority: so magnificence requires those capable of
great deeds, and purple calls for noble men; and, in the same way, the il-
lustrious vernacular demands writers of outstanding intelligence and
knowledge, and spurns all others, as will become clear below. For what- 6

47

digni, quidam digniores, quidam dignissimi esse possunt, manifestum est quod bona dignis, meliora dignioribus, optima dignissimis conve-

8 nient. Et cum loquela non aliter sit necessarium instrumentum nostre conceptionis quam equus militis, et optimis militibus optimi conveniant equi, ut dictum est, optimis conceptionibus optima loquela conveniet. Sed optime conceptiones non possunt esse nisi ubi scientia et ingenium est: ergo optima loquela non convenit nisi illis in quibus ingenium et scientia est. Et sic non omnibus versificantibus optima loquela conveniet, cum plerique sine scientia et ingenio versificentur, et per consequens nec optimum vulgare. Quapropter, si non omnibus competit, non omnes ipsum debent uti, quia inconvenienter agere nullus debet.

9 Et ubi dicitur quod quilibet suos versus exornare debet in quantum potest, verum esse testamur; sed nec bovem epiphiatum nec balteatum suem dicemus ornatum, immo potius deturpatum ridemus illum: est

10 enim exornatio alicuius convenientis additio. Ad illud ubi dicitur quod superiora inferioribus admixta profectum adducunt, dicimus verum esse quando cesset discretio: puta si aurum cum argento conflemus; sed si discretio remanet, inferiora vilescunt: puta cum formose mulieres deformibus admiscentur. Unde cum sententia versificantium semper verbis discretive mixta remaneat, si non fuerit optima, optimo sociata vulgari non melior sed deterior apparebit, quemadmodum turpis mulier si auro vel serico vestiatur.

ever is suited to us is so because we belong to a genus, or a species, or because we are who we are: this is true, for instance, of our having sense-perceptions, or laughing, or riding a horse.[101] But the illustrious vernacular is not suited to us because we belong to a genus – otherwise it would also be suited to brute beasts; nor because we belong to a species – otherwise it would be suited to every human being, which is unthinkable (for no one would suggest that it is appropriate for mountain-dwellers discussing country matters); so it must be suited to us as individuals. But nothing suits an individual except in respect of the par- 7 ticular qualities that he possesses, as in the cases of carrying on a trade, or riding a horse, or governing. Therefore, if the various degrees of suitability reflect qualities, as they do in worthy individuals, so that some are worthy, some worthier, and some most worthy, it is clear that good things are suited to the worthy, better to the more worthy, and the best to the most worthy. And since language is nothing other than the 8 vehicle indispensable to our thinking, as a horse is to a knight, and since the best horses are suited to the best knights, as I said, the best language is suited to the best thinking. But the best thinking is not to be found except where knowledge and intelligence are also present; therefore the best language is suited only to those who possess intelligence and knowledge. And so the best language is not suitable for all versifiers, since most of them write their verses without knowledge or intelligence; and, as a consequence, the best type of vernacular is not suitable for them either. On this account, if the illustrious vernacular is not appropriate for all, then not everyone should use it, since no one should do anything that is inappropriate.

And as for my remark that anyone should embellish his lines as 9 much as he can, I declare that this is true; but we would not call an ox well-adorned if it were dressed up to look like a horse, or a sow if it wore a sword-belt – rather, we would laugh at their disfiguring get-up, for true adornment consists in the addition of something appropriate. As for the 10 point that superior material mixed with inferior enhances the inferior, I say that this is true when the distinction between the two is lost, as when gold is blended with silver; but if the distinction survives, then the inferior material actually loses value, as when beautiful women are seen in the company of ugly ones. So, since poets' thought is mixed with their words but can always be distinguished from them, when that thought is not of the best it will not seem better for being mixed with the best type of vernacular, but worse – as would an ugly woman swathed in gold or silk.

II

1   Postquam non omnes versificantes sed tantum excellentissimos illustre uti vulgare debere astruximus, consequens est astruere utrum omnia ipso tractanda sint aut non: et si non omnia, que ipso digna sunt segregatim ostendere.

2   Circa quod primo reperiendum est id quod intelligimus per illud quod dicimus dignum. Et dicimus dignum esse quod dignitatem habet, sicut nobile quod nobilitatem; et si cognito habituante habituatum cognoscitur in quantum huiusmodi, cognita dignitate cognoscemus et

3   dignum. Est etenim dignitas meritorum effectus sive terminus; ut, cum quis bene meruit, ad boni dignitatem profectum esse dicimus, cum male vero, ad mali: puta bene militantem ad victorie dignitatem, bene autem regentem ad regni, nec non mendacem ad ruboris dignitatem, et la-

4   tronem ad eam que est mortis. Sed cum in bene merentibus fiant comparationes, et in aliis etiam, ut quidam bene quidam melius quidam optime, quidam male quidam peius quidam pessime mereantur, et huiusmodi comparationes non fiant nisi per respectum ad terminum meritorum, quem dignitatem dicimus, ut dictum est, manifestum est ut dignitates inter se comparentur secundum magis et minus, ut quedam magne, quedam maiores, quedam maxime sint; et per consequens aliquid

5   dignum, aliquid dignius, aliquid dignissimum esse constat. Et cum comparatio dignitatum non fiat circa idem obiectum, sed circa diversa, ut dignius dicamus quod maioribus, dignissimum quod maximis dignum est (quia nichil eodem dignius esse potest), manifestum est quod optima optimis secundum rerum exigentiam digna sunt. Unde cum hoc quod dicimus illustre sit optimum aliorum vulgarium, consequens est ut sola optima digna sint ipso tractari, que quidem tractandorum dignissima nuncupamus.

6   Nunc autem que sint ipsa venemur. Ad quorum evidentiam sciendum est quod sicut homo tripliciter spirituatus est, videlicet vegetabili, animali et rationali, triplex iter perambulat. Nam secundum quod vegetabile quid est, utile querit, in quo cum plantis comunicat; secundum quod animale, delectabile, in quo cum brutis; secundum quod rationale, honestum querit, in quo solus est, vel angelice sociatur ‹nature›. Propter hec tria quicquid agimus agere videmur; et quia in quolibet istorum quedam sunt maiora quedam maxima, secundum quod talia, que maxima sunt maxime pertractanda videntur, et per consequens maximo vulgari.

7   Sed disserendum est que maxima sint. Et primo in eo quod est utile: in quo, si callide consideremus intentum omnium querentium utili-

II

Now that I have explained that not all poets, but only the very best of them, should use the illustrious vernacular, it becomes necessary to establish whether or not it can be used to discuss all subjects; and, if not, to show separately which subjects are worthy of it. 1

To this end, it will first be necessary to decide what we mean when we say something is 'worthy'. Now we call 'worthy' that which possesses worthiness, as we do 'noble' that which possesses nobility; and if, having learned to recognise distinguishing features, we can recognise the object they distinguish in so far as it is of its kind, so, having learned to recognise worthiness, we shall also be able to recognise what is worthy. 2

Worthiness is, in fact, the effect or culmination of what one has deserved; so that, when someone has deserved well of us, we say that he has achieved worthiness of good, or, if the contrary is true, of evil. So a good soldier achieves worthiness of victory, or a good ruler of his kingdom, just as a liar achieves worthiness of shame or a thief of death. But, since 3

comparisons can be made among those who have deserved well (as well as among others), so that some deserve well, some better, and some the best (or some badly, some worse, and some the worst), and since comparisons of this kind can only be made on the basis of the culmination of merit that we call worthiness (as has been said), it is plain that degrees of worthiness, greater and lesser, can be established by comparing them with each other, so that some are great, some greater, and some greatest. It follows that some things are worthy, some worthier, and some most worthy. And since this comparison of degrees of worthiness is not 4

applied to a single object, but to different ones, so that we can call 'worthier' what is worthy of greater things and 'most worthy' what is worthy of the greatest (because nothing can be worthier of the same), it is clear that the best is worthy of the best, according to the intrinsic nature of things. So since the vernacular I call illustrious is the best of all vernaculars, it follows that only the best subjects are worthy to be discussed in it, and those, of the subjects that can be discussed, are the ones we call most worthy. 5

Now, however, let us track down what they are. In order to define them accurately, it is necessary first to know that, just as human beings possess a soul with three aspects – vegetative, animal, and rational – so they follow a threefold path. For in so far as they are vegetable beings, they seek the useful, and they have this in common with plants; in so far as they are animal, they seek pleasure, and this they share with beasts; and in so far as they are rational, they seek the good, and in this they 6

tatem, nil aliud quam salutem inveniemus. Secundo in eo quod est delectabile: in quo dicimus illud esse maxime delectabile quod per pretiosissimum obiectum appetitus delectat: hoc autem venus est. Tertio in eo quod est honestum: in quo nemo dubitat esse virtutem. Quare hec tria, salus videlicet, venus et virtus, apparent esse illa magnalia que sint maxime pertractanda, hoc est ea que maxime sunt ad ista, ut armorum probitas, amoris accensio et directio voluntatis. Circa que sola, si bene recolimus, illustres viros invenimus vulgariter poetasse, scilicet Bertramum de Bornio arma, Arnaldum Danielem amorem, Gerardum de Bornello rectitudinem; Cynum Pistoriensem amorem, amicum eius rectitudinem. Bertramus etenim ait

Non posc mudar c'un cantar non exparia

Arnaldus:

L'aura amara
fa.l bruol brancuz
clarzir;

Gerardus:

Per solaz reveilar
che s'es trop endormiz;

Cynus:

Digno sono eo di morte;

amicus eius:

Doglia mi reca ne lo core ardire.

Arma vero nullum latium adhuc invenio poetasse.

Hiis proinde visis, que canenda sint vulgari altissimo innotescunt.

stand alone, or may be related to the nature of angels. Clearly, it is in pursuit of these three ends that we do whatever we do; and because in each area there are some things of greater importance and some of greatest, they are to be treated according to their importance, the most important in the loftiest mode and, therefore, in the highest form of vernacular.

But we must discuss what these things of greatest importance may 7 be. To begin with what is useful: here, if we carefully ponder the goal of all those who seek what is useful, we will find that it is nothing other than their own well-being. Secondly, what is pleasurable: here I say that what is most pleasurable is what is the most highly valued object of our desires; and this is love. Thirdly, what is good: and here no-one will doubt that the most important thing is virtue. So these three things, well-being, love, and virtue, appear to be those most important subjects that are to be treated in the loftiest style; or at least this is true of the themes most closely associated with them, prowess in arms, ardour in love, and control of one's own will. On these themes alone, if I remember 8 rightly, we find that illustrious individuals have written poetry in the vernacular: Bertran de Born on arms, Arnaut Daniel on love, Giraut de Borneil on integrity; Cino da Pistoia on love, his friend on integrity. So Bertran says:

Non posc mudar c'un cantar non exparia;[102]

Arnaut:

L'aura amara
fa.l bruol brancuz
clarzir[103]

Giraut:

Per solaz reveilar
che s'es trop endormiz;[104]

Cino:

Digno sono eo di morte;[105]

his friend:

Doglia mi reca ne lo core ardire.[106]

As for arms, I find that no Italian has yet treated them in poetry.

Having seen this, then, the subjects fit for poetry in the highest form 9 of vernacular will become clear.

III

1   Nunc autem quo modo ea coartare debemus que tanto sunt digna vulgari, sollicite investigare conemur.

2   Volentes igitur modum tradere quo ligari hec digna existant, primo dicimus esse ad memoriam reducendum quod vulgariter poetantes sua poemata multimode protulerunt, quidam per cantiones, quidam per ballatas, quidam per sonitus, quidam per alios inlegitimos et inregulares

3   modos, ut inferius ostendetur. Horum autem modorum cantionum modum excellentissimum putamus: quare si excellentissima excellentissimis digna sunt, ut superius est probatum, illa que excellentissimo sunt digna vulgari, modo excellentissimo digna sunt, et per consequens in cantionibus pertractanda.

4   Quod autem modus cantionum sit talis ut dictum est, pluribus potest rationibus indagari. Prima quidem quia, cum quicquid versificamur sit cantio, sole cantiones hoc vocabulum sibi sortite sunt: quod nunquam

5   sine vetusta provisone processit. Adhuc: quicquid per se ipsum efficit illud ad quod factum est, nobilius esse videtur quam quod extrinseco indiget; sed cantiones per se totum quod debent efficiunt, quod ballate non faciunt – indigent enim plausoribus, ad quos edite sunt: ergo cantiones nobiliores ballatis esse sequitur extimandas, et per consequens nobilissimum aliorum esse modum illarum, cum nemo dubitet quin

6   ballate sonitus nobilitate modi excellant. Preterea: illa videntur nobiliora esse que conditori suo magis honoris afferunt; sed cantiones magis deferunt suis conditoribus quam ballate: igitur nobiliores sunt, et per con-

7   sequens modus earum nobilissimus aliorum. Preterea: que nobilissima sunt carissime conservantur; sed inter ea que cantata sunt, cantiones carissime conservantur, ut constat visitantibus libros: ergo cantiones

8   nobilissime sunt, et per consequens modus earum nobilissimus est. Ad hoc: in artificiatis illud est nobilissimum quod totam comprehendit artem; cum igitur ea que cantantur artificiata existant, et in solis cantionibus ars tota comprehendatur, cantiones nobilissime sunt, et sic modus earum nobilissimus aliorum. Quod autem tota comprehendatur in cantionibus ars cantandi poetice, in hoc palatur, quod quicquid artis reperitur in omnibus aliis, et in cantionibus reperitur; sed non convertitur

9   hoc. Signum autem horum que dicimus promptum in conspectu habetur: nam quicquid de cacuminibus illustrium capitum poetantium profluxit ad labia, in solis cantionibus invenitur.

10   Quare ad propositum patet quod ea que digna sunt vulgari altissimo in cantionibus tractanda sunt.

III

Now, however, let us quickly try to find out how the themes that are 1
worthy of such a vernacular are to be constrained.

Wishing, then, to explain how these worthy themes are to be con- 2
nected in poetry, I shall first say that it ought to be remembered that
writers of poetry in the vernacular have composed their poems using
many different forms, some writing *canzoni*, some *ballate*, some sonnets,
and some using other illegitimate and irregular forms, as will be shown
below. Of all these forms, however, I hold[107] that the *canzone* form is far 3
and away the most excellent; and so, if excellent things are worthy of the
excellent, as was proved above, those subjects that are worthy of the most
excellent vernacular are also worthy of the most excellent form, and, in
consequence, are to be treated in the *canzone*.

That the *canzone* form is everything I have said can be shown using a 4
number of arguments. First, that although everything composed in verse
involves song, only *canzoni* have had that term allotted to them – which
could not have happened without ancient authority. Further, everything 5
that brings about unaided the purpose for which it was created is seen as
more noble than that which requires outside help; and *canzoni* do every-
thing that they need to do unaided, unlike *ballate* – for those need
dancers, for whom they were written in the first place. It follows, there-
fore, that *canzoni* are to be deemed more noble than *ballate*; and, as a
result, their form is the most noble of all, since no one doubts that *ballate*
excel sonnets in point of nobility of form. Moreover, those things are seen 6
as more noble that bring greater honour to those who create them; but
canzoni bring more honour to their creators than *ballate*; therefore they
are more noble, and, in consequence, theirs is the noblest form of all.
Furthermore, the noblest things are preserved with the greatest care; 7
but, among the things that are sung, *canzoni* are preserved the most care-
fully, as is clear to anyone who looks at books; therefore, *canzoni* are most
noble, and theirs is the noblest of forms. Yet further, among the products 8
of human ingenuity, the noblest are those that most fully exploit the tech-
nical possibilities of the art; since things that are sung are products of
human ingenuity, and only in *canzoni* are the technical possibilities of
the art fully exploited, so *canzoni* are most noble, and the noblest of poetic
forms. That the technical possibilities of singing in poetry are fully
exploited only in *canzoni* is apparent from the fact that whatever features
of the art are found in other forms are also found in *canzoni* – but the con-
verse is not true. Proof of what I am arguing is readily available: for what- 9

IV

1 Quando quidem aporiavimus extricantes qui sint aulico digni vulgari et que, nec non modum quem tanto dignamur honore ut solus altissimo vulgari conveniat, antequam migremus ad alia modum cantionum, quem casu magis quam arte multi usurpare videntur, enucleemus; et qui hucusque casualiter est assumptus, illius artis ergasterium reseremus, modum ballatarum et sonituum ommictentes, quia illum elucidare intendimus in quarto huius operis, cum de mediocri vulgari tractabimus.

2 Revisentes igitur ea que dicta sunt, recolimus nos eos qui vulgariter versificantur plerunque vocasse poetas: quod procul dubio rationabiliter eructare presumpsimus, quia prorsus poete sunt, si poesim recte consid-

3 eremus: que nichil aliud est quam fictio rethorica musicaque poita. Differunt tamen a magnis poetis, hoc est regularibus, quia magni sermone et arte regulari poetati sunt, hii vero casu, ut dictum est. Idcirco accidit ut, quantum illos proximius imitemur, tantum rectius poetemur. Unde nos doctrine operi intendentes, doctrinatas eorum poetrias emulari oportet.

4 Ante omnia ergo dicimus unumquenque debere materie pondus propriis humeris coequare, ne forte humerorum nimio gravata virtute in cenum cespitare necesse sit: hoc est quod Magister noster Oratius precipit cum in principio Poetrie 'Sumite materiam' dicit.

5 Deinde in hiis que dicenda occurrunt debemus discretione potiri, utrum tragice, sive comice, sive elegiace sint canenda. Per tragediam superiorem stilum inducimus, per comediam inferiorem, per elegiam

6 stilum intelligimus miserorum. Si tragice canenda videntur, tunc assumendum est vulgare illustre, et per consequens cantionem ligare. Si vero comice, tunc quandoque mediocre quandoque humile vulgare sumatur: et huius discretionem in quarto huius reservamus ostendere. Si autem elegiace, solum humile oportet nos sumere.

7 Sed ommictamus alios, et nunc, ut conveniens est, de stilo tragico pertractemus. Stilo equidem tragico tunc uti videmur quando cum gravitate sententie tam superbia carminum quam constructionis elatio et excel-

8 lentia vocabulorum concordat. Quare, si bene recolimus summa summis esse digna iam fuisse probatum, et iste quem tragicum appellamus summus videtur esse stilorum, illa que summe canenda distinximus isto

ever has flowed down to the lips of illustrious poets from the loftiest reaches of their minds is found only in *canzoni*.'

So for our purposes it is plain that whatever is worthy of the highest 10 form of the vernacular should be treated in *canzoni*.

IV

Now that I have, not without difficulty, elucidated some tricky pro- 1 blems – who and what is worthy of the aulic vernacular, as well as which form I consider worthy of such honour as, alone, to be suited for the vernacular at its highest – I wish, before moving on to other matters, to enquire thoroughly into the *canzone* form, which many clearly employ more at random than according to the rules; and since, so far, all this has been taken for granted, I will now throw open the workshop of that art (leaving the forms of *ballata* and sonnet aside for the moment, since I plan to explain them in the fourth book of the present work, which will deal with the middle level of the vernacular).

Looking back, then, at what was said above, I recall that I frequently 2 called those who write verse in the vernacular 'poets'; and this presumptuous expression is beyond question justifiable, since they are most certainly poets, if we understand poetry aright: that is, as nothing other than a verbal invention composed according to the rules of rhetoric and music. Yet they differ from the great poets, that is, those who obey the 3 rules,[108] since those great ones wrote their poetry in a language, and with a technique, governed by rules, whereas these write at random, as I said above. Thus it comes about that, the more closely we try to imitate the great poets, the more correctly we write poetry. So, since I am trying to write a theoretical work about poetry, it behoves me to emulate their learned works of poetic doctrine.

First of all I declare that anyone must adjust the weight of his material 4 to suit his own shoulders, lest the excessive burden bearing down upon them overcome his strength and send him sprawling in the mud; and this is what our master Horace teaches at the beginning of his *Ars poetica*, where he says 'Choose your subject.'[109]

Then, when dealing with the various subjects that are suitable for 5 poetry, we must know how to choose whether to treat them in tragic, comic, or elegiac style. By 'tragic' I mean the higher style, by 'comic' the lower, and by 'elegiac' that of the unhappy. If it seems appropriate to use 6 the tragic style, then the illustrious vernacular must be employed, and so you will need to bind together a *canzone*. If, on the other hand, the comic style is called for, then sometimes the middle level of the vernacular can

solo sunt stilo canenda: videlicet salus, amor et virtus et que propter ea concipimus, dum nullo accidente vilescant.

9   Caveat ergo quilibet et discernat ea que dicimus, et quando pure hec tria cantare intendit, vel que ad ea directe ac pure secuntur, prius Elicone potatus, tensis fidibus ad supremum, secure plectrum tum movere inci-
10 piat. Sed cautionem atque discretionem hanc accipere, sicut decet, hic opus et labor est, quoniam nunquam sine strenuitate ingenii et artis assiduitate scientiarumque habitu fieri potest. Et hii sunt quos Poeta Eneidorum sexto Dei dilectos et ab ardente virtute sublimatos ad ethera
11 deorumque filios vocat, quanquam figurate loquatur. Et ideo confutetur illorum stultitia qui, arte scientiaque immunes, de solo ingenio confidentes, ad summa summe canenda prorumpunt; et a tanta presumptuositate desistant; et si anseres natura vel desidia sunt, nolint astripetam aquilam imitari.

V

1   De gravitate sententiarum vel satis dixisse videmur vel saltim totum quod operis est nostri: quapropter ad superbiam carminum festinemus.

2   Circa quod sciendum quod predecessores nostri diversis carminibus usi sunt in cantionibus suis, quod et moderni faciunt, sed nullum adhuc invenimus in carmen sillabicando endecadem transcendisse, nec a trisillabo descendisse. Et licet trisillabo carmine atque endecasillabo et omnibus intermediis cantores latii usi sint, pentasillabum et eptasil-

be used, and sometimes the lowly; and I shall explain the distinction in Book Four. If, though, you are writing elegy, you must only use the lowly.

But let us leave the other styles aside and, as is appropriate, discuss 7 only the tragic here. The tragic style is clearly to be used whenever both the magnificence of the verses and the lofty excellence of construction and vocabulary accord with the gravity of the subject-matter. Therefore, 8 remembering well that (as has been proved above) whatever is highest is worthy of the highest, and seeing that the style we call 'tragic' is the highest kind of style, the subjects that we have defined as requiring to be treated in the highest style must be treated in that style alone. And those subjects are well-being, love, and virtue, and the thoughts that they inspire in us, as long as no accidental circumstance intervenes to defile them.

Let everyone, then, take care to understand precisely what I am 9 stating; and, if they still undertake to write poetry purely on these three themes, or on themes that flow directly and purely from them, let them first drink deep of Helicon[110], and tighten their strings to the utmost, and they will then be able to wield the plectrum with absolute confidence. But learning the necessary caution and discernment is 'the difficult part, 10 requiring much effort',[111] since these can never be achieved without exertion of the intellect, dedicated study of technique, and immersion in knowledge. And those who succeed are those whom the author of the *Aeneid*, in the sixth book, calls God's beloved, raised to the heavens by their ardent virtue and made the children of God – though he is speaking figuratively.[112] And this should suffice to refute the foolish claims of those 11 who, devoid of technique and knowledge, relying on ingenuity alone, lay hands on the noblest topics, those that should be sung in the highest style. Let them lay such presumption aside; and, if nature or their own incompetence has made them geese, let them not try to emulate the star-seeking[113] eagle.

V

It seems to me that enough has now been said as to the gravity of 1 subject-matter, or at least as much as is relevant for the purpose of my work, so I shall move quickly on to the magnificence of the verses.

On this topic it must first be realised that our predecessors used lines 2 of varying lengths in their *canzoni*, as do our contemporaries; but I have not yet found any case in which the number of syllables in a single line exceeds eleven or falls short of three. And although Italian poets have

labum et endecasillabum in usu frequentiori habentur, et post hec trisillabum ante alia.

3   Quorum omnium endecasillabum videtur esse superbius, tam temporis occupatione quam capacitate sententie, constructionis et vocabulorum; quorum omnium specimen magis multiplicatur in illo, ut manifeste apparet: nam ubicunque ponderosa multiplicantur,   et

4   pondus. Et hoc omnes doctores perpendisse videntur, cantiones illustres principiantes ab illo; ut Gerardus de B.:

Ara ausirez encabalitz cantarz

(quod carmen, licet decasillabum videatur, secundum rei veritatem endecasillabum est: nam due consonantes extreme non sunt de sillaba precedente, et licet propriam vocalem non habeant, virtutem sillabe non tamen ammictunt; signum autem est quod rithimus ibi una vocali perficitur, quod esse non posset nisi virtute alterius ibi subintellecte); Rex Navarre:

De fin amor si vient sen et bonté

(ubi, si consideretur accentus et eius causa, endecasillabum esse constabit); Guido Guinizelli:

Al cor gentil repara sempre amore;

Iudex de Columpnis de Messana:

Amor, che lungiamente m'hai menato;

Renaldus de Aquino:

Per fino amore vo si letamente;

Cynus Pistoriensis:

Non spero che giamai per mia salute;

amicus eius:

Amor, che movi tua virtù da cielo.

5   Et licet hoc quod dictum est celeberrimum carmen, ut dignum est, videatur omnium aliorum, si eptasillabi aliqualem societatem assumat, dummodo principatum obtineat, clarius magisque sursum superbire

6   videtur. Sed hoc ulterius elucidandum remaneat. Et dicimus eptasillabum sequi illud quod maximum est in celebritate. Post hoc pentasillabum et deinde trisillabum ordinamus. Neasillabum vero, quia triplicatum trisillabum videbatur, vel nunquam in honore fuit vel

used trisyllabic lines, and hendecasyllables, and every type of line in between, the most popular have been the lines of five, seven, and eleven syllables, with the trisyllable most favoured among those that remain.

Of all these lines the most splendid is clearly the hendecasyllable, 3 both for its measured movement and for the scope it offers for subject-matter, constructions, and vocabulary; and the beauty of all these features is most greatly magnified by this metre, as will be readily apparent: for whenever things of value are magnified, their value itself is magnified also. And all the best poets seem to have accepted this, and have begun 4 their illustrious *canzoni* with a hendecasyllable. Thus Giraut de B.:

Ara ausirez encabalitz cantarz[114]

(Though this line may appear to have only ten syllables, it is, in fact, a hendecasyllable, for the two final consonants do not belong to the preceding syllable, and although they have no vowel of their own, they do not lose their value as syllables on that account. The proof of this is that here the rhyme is completed with a single vowel, which would not be possible except by virtue of another whose presence here is understood.) The King of Navarre:

De fin amor si vient sen et bonté[115]

(Here, if we take stress and its motivation into account, it will be clear that this is a hendecasyllable.)[116] Guido Guinizzelli:

Al cor gentil repara sempre amore;[117]

Delle Colonne, the judge of Messina:

Amor, che lungiamente m'hai menato;[118]

Rinaldo d'Aquino:

Per fino amor vo si letamente;[119]

Cino da Pistoia:

Non spero che giamai per mia salute;[120]

and his friend:

Amor, che movi tua virtù da cielo.[121]

And although this line I have been discussing is rightly seen as the 5 most celebrated of all, should it enter into a kind of co-operative bond with the seven-syllable line, or heptasyllable (where it still retains, as it were, the senior partnership), it will appear yet more exalted and distin-

7 propter fastidium absolevit. Parisillabis vero propter sui ruditatem non
utimur nisi raro: retinent enim naturam suorum numerorum, qui
numeris imparibus quemadmodum materia forme subsistunt.

Et sic, recolligentes predicta, endecasillabum videtur esse superbis-
8 simum carmen: et hoc est quod querebamus. Nunc autem restat investi-
gandum de constructionibus elatis et fastigiosis vocabulis; et demum,
fustibus torquibusque paratis, promissum fascem, hoc est cantionem,
quo modo viere quis debeat instruemus.

VI

Quia circa vulgare illustre nostra versatur intentio, quod nobilis-
1 simum est aliorum, et ea que digna sunt illo cantari discrevimus, que tria
nobilissima sunt, ut superius est astructum, et modum cantionarium se-
legimus illis, tanquam aliorum modorum summum, et, ut ipsum perfec-
tius edocere possimus, quedam iam preparavimus, stilum videlicet atque
carmen, nunc de constructione agamus.

Est enim sciendum quod constructionem vocamus regulatam compa-
2 ginem dictionum, ut 'Aristotiles phylosophatus est tempore Alexandri'.
Sunt enim quinque hic dictiones compacte regulariter, et unam faciunt
3 constructionem. Circa hanc quidem prius considerandum est quod con-
structionum alia congrua est, alia vero incongrua. Et quia, si primordium
bene discretionis nostre recolimus, sola supprema venamur, nullum in
nostra venatione locum habet incongrua, quia nec inferiorem gradum
bonitatis promeruit. Pudeat ergo, pudeat ydiotas tantum audere dein-
ceps ut ad cantiones prorumpant: quos non aliter deridemus quam
cecum de coloribus distinguentem. Est ut videtur congrua quam sec-
tamur.

Sed non minoris difficultatis accedit discretio priusquam quam quer-
4 imus actingamus, videlicet urbanitate plenissimam. Sunt etenim gradus
constructionum quamplures: videlicet insipidus, qui est rudium, ut
'Petrus amat multum dominam Bertam'; est et pure sapidus, qui est rigi-
dorum scolarium vel magistrorum, ut 'Piget me cunctis pietate maiorem,
quicunque in exilio tabescentes patriam tantum sompniando revisunt';

guished in its pride. But let me leave this point to be developed later on.   6
And I say that the heptasyllable comes immediately after this line, which
reaches the highest peak of celebrity. After this I would place the five-syl-
lable line, or pentasyllable, and the trisyllable. The nine-syllable line, on
the other hand, being a kind of threefold trisyllable, has either never been
highly thought of or has dropped out of use because it was found boring.
Lines with an even number of syllables are only used rarely today   7
because of their lack of sophistication; for they retain the nature of the
numbers that govern them, which are inferior to odd numbers as mate-
rial is to form.

And so, to recapitulate what has been said, the hendecasyllable may   8
be seen as the most splendid of lines; and this is what we were trying to
determine. Now, however, we must still explore the question of lofty con-
structions and refined vocabulary; and then, once the sticks and the
cords have been gathered, I shall explain how our promised bundle, the
canzone, is to be bound together.

VI

Since the object of my attention is the illustrious vernacular, which is   1
the noblest of all, and since I have determined what are the subjects
worthy of that vernacular – the three noblest subjects, as explained
above – and have reserved for them the form of the *canzone*, as being the
greatest of all forms, and since, in order to teach the use of that form more
thoroughly, I have dealt above with some aspects of it, namely its style
and its metre, let us now turn to the matter of construction.

You need to know that we call 'construction' a group of words put to-   2
gether in regulated order, such as 'Aristotle philosophised in Alexander's
time'. Here we have, in fact, five words arranged in a regular fashion, and   3
they make up one construction. On this subject it must first be taken into
account that some constructions are congruent, and some, on the other
hand, incongruent. And since, as you should well recall from our prin-
ciple of distinction, we are hunting only for the best, there is no place on
our expedition for the incongruent type of construction, because it has
not been awarded even the lowest place on the scale of quality. Let the ig-
norant, then, not dare from now on to lay rough hands on *canzoni*; for we
laugh at them as we would at a blind man choosing among colours. It is,
as will be plain, the congruent construction that we pursue.   4

But a distinction no less tricky than this must be made before we can
find what we seek, which is the construction with the highest possible
degree of urbanity. For there are many degrees of construction. There is

est et sapidus et venustus, qui est quorundam superficietenus rethoricam aurientium, ut 'Laudabilis discretio marchionis Estensis, et sua magnificentia preparata, cunctis illum facit esse dilectum'; est et sapidus et venustus etiam et excelsus, qui est dictatorum illustrium, ut 'Eiecta maxima parte florum de sinu tuo, Florentia, nequicquam Trinacriam Totila secundus adivit'. Hunc gradum constructionis excellentissimum nominamus, et hic est quem querimus cum supprema venemur, ut dictum est.

5

Hoc solum illustres cantiones inveniuntur contexte, ut Gerardus:

6

Si per mos Sobretos non fos;

Folquetus de Marsilia:

Tan m'abellis l'amoros pensamen;

Arnaldus Danielis:

Sols sui che sai lo sobraffan che.m sorz;

Namericus de Belnui:

Nuls hom non pot complir addreciamen;

Namericus de Peculiano:

Si con l'arbres che per sobrecarcar;

Rex Navarre:

Ire d'amor que en mon cor repaire;

Iudex de Messana:

Ancor che l'aigua per lo foco lassi;

Guido Guinizelli:

Tegno de folle empresa a lo ver dire;

Guido Cavalcantis:

Poi che di doglia cor conven ch'io porti;

Cynus de Pistorio:

Avegna che io aggia più per tempo;

amicus eius:

Amor che ne la mente mi ragiona.

the flavourless, for example, which is typical of the uncultured: 'Peter loves Miss Bertha a lot.'[122] There is one that is, flavoured and no more, typical of pedantic students and teachers: 'I am stricken with sorrow more than most, for whomever drags out his life in exile, revisiting his native land only in dreams.' There is one that is graceful as well as flavoured, which is found among those who have made a superficial study of rhetoric: 'The laudable discretion of the Marquis of Este, and his widely displayed generosity, make him beloved of all.' And there is the flavoured one that is graceful and also striking, and this is typical of illustrious writers: 'The greater part of your flowers, o Florence, having been snatched from your breast, the second Totila advanced in vain towards Trinacria.' This is the degree of construction that I call most excellent, 5 and this is what we are looking for when we hunt the best, as I said.

Illustrious *canzoni* are composed using this type of construction 6 alone, as in this one by Giraut:

Si per mos Sobretos non fos;[123]

Folquet de Marselha:

Tan m'abellis l'amoros pensamen;[124]

Arnaut Daniel:

Sols sui che sai lo sobraffan che.m sorz;[125]

Aimeric de Belenoi:

Nuls hom non pot complir addreciamen;[126]

Aimeric de Peguilhan:

Si con l'arbres che per sobrecarcar;[127]

The King of Navarre:

Ire d'amor que en mon cor repaire;[128]

The Judge of Messina:

Ancòr che l'aigua per lo foco lassi;[129]

Guido Guinizzelli:

Tegno de folle empresa a lo ver dire;[130]

Guido Cavalcanti:

Poi che di doglia cor conven ch'io porti;[131]

7   Nec mireris, lector, de tot reductis autoribus ad memoriam: non enim hanc quam suppremam vocamus constructionem nisi per huiusmodi exempla possumus indicare. Et fortassis utilissimum foret ad illam habituandam regulatos vidisse poetas, Virgilium videlicet, Ovidium Metamorfoseos, Statium atque Lucanum, nec non alios qui usi sunt altissimas prosas, ut Titum Livium, Plinium, Frontinum, Paulum Orosium, et
8   multos alios quos amica sollicitudo nos visitare invitat. Subsistant igitur ignorantie sectatores Guictonem Aretinum et quosdam alios extollentes, nunquam in vocabulis atque constructione plebescere desuetos.

VII

1   Grandiosa modo vocabula sub prelato stilo digna consistere, successiva nostre progressionis presentia lucidari expostulat.
2   Testamur proinde incipientes non minimum opus esse rationis discretionem vocabulorum habere, quoniam perplures eorum maneries inveniri posse videmus. Nam vocabulorum quedam puerilia, quedam muliebria, quedam virilia; et horum quedam silvestria, quedam urbana; et eorum que urbana vocamus, quedam pexa et lubrica, quedam yrsuta et reburra sentimus. Inter que quidem, pexa atque yrsuta sunt illa que vocamus grandiosa, lubrica vero et reburra vocamus illa que in superfluum sonant; quemadmodum in magnis operibus quedam magnanimitatis sunt opera, quedam fumi: ubi, licet in superficie quidam consideretur ascensus, ex quo limitata virtutis linea prevaricatur, bone rationis non ascensus sed per altera declivia ruina constabit.
3   Intuearis ergo, lector, actente quantum ad exaceranda egregia verba te cribrare oportet: nam si vulgare illustre consideres, quo tragici debent uti poete vulgares, ut superius dictum est, quos informare intendimus,
4   sola vocabula nobilissima in cribro tuo residere curabis. In quorum numero nec puerilia propter sui simplicitatem ut *mamma* et *babbo*, *mate* et *pate*, nec muliebria propter sui mollitiem, ut *dolciada* et *placevole*, nec silvestria propter austeritatem, ut *greggia* et *cetra*, nec urbana lubrica et reburra, ut *femina* et *corpo*, ullo modo poteris conlocare. Sola etenim pexa

Cino da Pistoia:

Avegna che io aggia più per tempo;[132]

and his friend:

Amor che ne la mente mi ragiona.[133]

Nor should you be surprised, reader, if so many authorities are recalled 7
to your memory here; for I could not make clear what I mean by the
supreme degree of construction other than by providing examples of this
kind. And perhaps it would be most useful, in order to make the practice
of such constructions habitual, to read the poets who respect the rules,
namely Virgil, the Ovid of the *Metamorphoses*, Statius, and Lucan, as well
as others who have written excellent prose, such as Livy, Pliny, Frontinus,
Paulus Orosius, and many others whom an affectionate interest invites 8
us to consult.[134] So let the devotees of ignorance cease to cry up Guittone
d'Arezzo and others like him, for never, in either vocabulary or construc-
tion, have they been anything but commonplace.

VII

The next section of our progress through this subject now requires 1
me to comment on vocabulary, which should be sublime, and therefore
worthy to contribute to the style defined above.

I shall begin by admitting that classifying words is not the least de- 2
manding of the tasks that exercise our reason, since we can plainly see
that many varieties are to be found. For some words can be seen as infan-
tile, some as womanish, some as virile; and of the virile some are thought
rustic and some urbane; and of those we call urbane some are combed
and glossy, some shaggy and unkempt. Of all these it is the combed and
the shaggy that we call sublime, while calling glossy and unkempt those
that have a superfluity of resonance. In the same way, among major en-
terprises, some reveal greatness of spirit and some are smoke;[135] and
although to the superficial observer they may seem to offer a way
upwards, yet, as soon as they step aside from the line laid down by virtue,
it will be clear to the sensible that they lead not upwards but to a headlong
fall down the opposite slope.

You should pay careful attention, then, reader, to the work you have 3
in store in order to sift out the words of superior quality from the rest; for
if you concentrate on the illustrious vernacular, which tragic poets in the
vernacular should use, as explained above (and it is tragic poets that I
seek to train), you will take care that only the noblest of words remain in

yrsutaque urbana tibi restare videbis, que nobilissima sunt et membra
5 vulgaris illustris. Et pexa vocamus illa que, trisillaba vel vicinissima trisil-
labitati, sine aspiratione, sine accento acuto vel circumflexo, sine z vel x
duplicibus, sine duarum liquidarum geminatione vel positione in-
mediate post mutam, dolata quasi, loquentem cum quadam suavitate re-
linquunt: ut *amore, donna, disio, virtute, donare, letitia, salute, securtate,
defesa.*
6 Yrsuta quoque dicimus omnia preter hec que vel necessaria vel or-
nativa videntur vulgaris illustris. Et necessaria quidem appellamus
que campsare non possumus, ut quedam monosillaba, ut *sì, no, me, te,
se, a, e, i, o, u*, interiectiones et alia multa. Ornativa vero dicimus omnia
polisillaba que, mixta cum pexis, pulcram faciunt armoniam compa-
ginis, quamvis asperitatem habeant aspirationis et accentus et dupli-
cium et liquidarum et prolixitatis: ut *terra, honore, speranza, gravitate,
allevíato, impossibilità, impossibilitate, benaventuratissimo, inanimatissi-
mamente, disaventuratissimamente, sovramagnificentissimamente,* quod
endecasillabum est. Posset adhuc inveniri plurium sillabarum voca-
bulum sive verbum, sed quia capacitatem omnium nostrorum car-
minum superexcedit, rationi presenti non videtur obnoxium, sicut est
illud *honorificabilitudinitate,* quod duodena perficitur sillaba in vulgari
et in gramatica tredena perficitur in duobus obliquis.
7 Quomodo autem pexis yrsuta huiusmodi sint armonizanda per
metra, inferius instruendum relinquimus. Et que iam dicta sunt de fasti-
giositate vocabulorum ingenue discretioni sufficiant.

VIII

1 Preparatis fustibus torquibusque ad fascem, nunc fasciandi tempus in-
cumbit. Sed quia cuiuslibet operis cognitio precedere debet operationem,
velut signum ante ammissionem sagipte vel iaculi, primo et principaliter
qui sit iste fascis quem fasciare intendimus videamus.

your sieve. And among these you will not be able to make any room at 4
all for infantile words (such as *mamma* and *babbo*, or *mate* and *pate*),[136]
because of their simplicity; or for the womanish (like *dolciada* or *place-*
vole),[137] because of their yielding quality; or for the rustic (like *greggia*
and *cetra*),[138] because of their roughness; or for the urbane, smooth or
unkempt, like *femina* or *corpo*.[139] So you will see that all you have left are
urbane words that are combed or shaggy; these are the most noble, and
belong to the illustrious vernacular.[140] And I define as 'combed' those 5
words that, having three syllables (or very close to that number), and
neither aspiration, nor acute or circumflex accent, nor doubled *z* or *x*, nor
twinned liquid consonants, nor such consonants placed immediately
after a mute, instead seem, as it were, polished, and leave a certain sweet-
ness in the mouths of those who utter them: such as *amore, donna, disio,*
virtute, donare, letitia, salute, securtate, and *defesa*.[141]

By 'shaggy' I mean all words, except those defined above, that seem 6
either necessary or decorative when used in the illustrious vernacular.
And I call necessary all those words that we simply cannot do without,
such as monosyllables like *si, no, me, te, se, a, e, i, o, u'*, as well as exclama-
tions and many others.[142] As for 'decorative', I so call all polysyllabic
words that, when mixed with combed ones, make the harmony of the
whole structure beautiful, even though they may have some harshness
of aspiration, or accent, or doubled consonants, or liquid ones, or may
simply be too long: these are words like *terra, honore, speranza, gravitate,*
alleviato, impossibilità, impossibilitate, benaventuratissimo, inanimatissi-
mamente, disaventuratissimamente, and *sovramagnificentissimamente,*
which last is a hendecasyllable all on its own.[143] A word or term with
even more syllables might still be found, but, since it would exceed the .
limits of all the lines that we use, it would not be very useful for our
present purpose: one such is the well-known *honorificabilitudinitate,*
which is twelve syllables long in the vernacular, and reaches thirteen in
two oblique cases that exist in *gramatica*.[144]

As for the question of how shaggy words of this type are to be recon- 7
ciled with combed ones within a metrical form, I shall postpone instruc-
tion on that point until later. And now let what I have said about the
sublimity of words suffice for those with innate discernment.

VIII

Now that we have gathered the sticks and cords for our bundle, the time 1
has come to put the bundle together. But since understanding of any

2   Fascis iste igitur, si bene comminiscimur omnia prelibata, cantio est. Quapropter quid sit cantio videamus, et quid intelligimus cum dicimus
3   cantionem. Est enim cantio, secundum verum nominis significatum, ipse canendi actus vel passio, sicut lectio passio vel actus legendi. Sed divaricemus quod dictum est, utrum videlicet hec sit cantio prout est actus,
4   vel prout est passio. Et circa hoc considerandum est quod cantio dupliciter accipi potest: uno modo secundum quod fabricatur ab autore suo, et sic est actio – et secundum istum modum Virgilius primo Eneidorum dicit 'Arma virumque cano' –; alio modo secundum quod fabricata profertur vel ab autore vel ab alio quicunque sit, sive cum soni modulatione proferatur, sive non: et sic est passio. Nam tunc agitur, modo vero agere videtur in alium, et sic tunc alicuius actio, modo quoque passio alicuius videtur. Et quia prius agitur ipsa quam agat, magis, immo prorsus denominari videtur ab eo quod agitur, et est actio alicuius, quam ab eo quod agit in alios. Signum autem huius est quod nunquam dicimus 'Hec est cantio Petri' eo quod ipsam proferat, sed eo quod fabricaverit illam.
5   Preterea disserendum est utrum cantio dicatur fabricatio verborum armonizatorum, vel ipsa modulatio. Ad quod dicimus quod nunquam modulatio dicitur cantio, sed sonus, vel thonus, vel nota, vel melos. Nullus enim tibicen, vel organista, vel cytharedus melodiam suam cantionem vocat, nisi in quantum nupta est alicui cantioni; sed armonizantes verba opera sua cantiones vocant, et etiam talia verba in cartulis
6   absque prolatore iacentia cantiones vocamus. Et ideo cantio nichil aliud esse videtur quam actio completa dicentis verba modulationi armonizata: quapropter tam cantiones quas nunc tractamus, quam ballatas et sonitus et omnia cuiuscunque modi verba sunt armonizata vulgariter et
7   regulariter, cantiones esse dicemus. Sed quia sola vulgaria ventilamus, regulata linquentes, dicimus vulgarium poematum unum esse suppremum, quod per superexcellentiam cantionem vocamus: quod autem suppremum quid sit cantio, in tertio huius libri capitulo est probatum. Et quoniam quod diffinitum est pluribus generale videtur, resumentes diffinitum iam generale vocabulum per quasdam differentias solum quod
8   petimus distinguamus. Dicimus ergo quod cantio, in quantum per superexcellentiam dicitur, ut et nos querimus, est equalium stantiarum sine responsorio ad unam sententiam tragica coniugatio, ut nos ostendimus cum dicimus

Donne ch'avete intelletto d'amore

Quod autem dicimus 'tragica coniugatio' est quia, cum comice fiat hec coniugatio, cantilenam vocamus per diminutionem: de qua in quarto huius tractare intendimus.

operation should be achieved before it is carried out, just as you should be able to see your target before you shoot an arrow or throw a javelin, let us consider, first and primarily, exactly what this bundle that I intend to put together may be.

This bundle, then, if we recall to mind all the evidence laid out above, is the *canzone*. Let us therefore find out what a *canzone* is, and what we mean when we say '*canzone*'. A *canzone*, according to the true meaning of the word *cantio*, is an act of singing, in an active or passive sense, just as *lectio* means an act of reading, in an active or passive sense. But let me define more precisely what I have just said, according, that is, to whether this act of singing is active or passive. And on this point it must be taken into account that *cantio* has a double meaning: one usage refers to something created by an author, so that there is action – and this is the sense in which Virgil uses the word in the first book of the *Aeneid*, when he writes '*arma virumque cano*';[145] the other refers to the occasions on which this creation is performed, either by the author or by someone else, whoever it may be, with or without a musical accompaniment – and in this sense it is passive. For on such occasions the *canzone* itself acts upon someone or something, whereas in the former case it is acted upon; and so in one case it appears as an action carried out by someone, in the other as an action perceived by someone. And because it is acted upon before it acts in its turn, the argument seems plausible, indeed convincing, that it takes its name from the fact that it is acted upon, and is somebody's action, rather than from the fact that it acts upon others. The proof of this is the fact that we never say 'that's Peter's song' when referring to something Peter has performed, but only to something he has written.

Furthermore, we must now discuss whether the word *canzone* should be used to refer to a composition made up of words arranged with due regard to harmony, or simply to a piece of music. To which I answer that a piece of music as such is never given the name *canzone*, but is rather called 'sound', or 'tone', or 'note', or 'melody'. For no player of a wind or keyboard or stringed instrument ever calls his melody a *canzone*, except when it is wedded to a real *canzone*; but those who harmonise words call their works *canzoni*, and even when we see such words written down on the page, in the absence of any performer, we call them *canzoni*. And so it seems clear that the *canzone* is nothing else than the self-contained action of one who writes harmonious words to be set to music; and so I shall assert that not only the *canzoni* we are discussing here, but also *ballate* and sonnets and all arrangements of words, of whatever kind, that are based on harmony, whether in the vernacular or in the regulated language, should be called *canzoni*. But because I am concerned here

2

3

4

5

6

7

9   Et sic patet quid cantio sit, et prout accipitur generaliter et prout per superexcellentiam vocamus eam. Satis etiam patere videtur quid intelligimus cum cantionem vocamus, et per consequens quid sit ille fascis quem ligare molimur.

IX

1   Quia, ut dictum est, cantio est coniugatio stantiarum, ignorato quid sit stantia necesse est cantionem ignorare: nam ex diffinientium cognitione diffiniti resultat cognitio; et ideo consequenter de stantia est agendum, ut scilicet investigemus quid ipsa sit, et quid per eam intelligere volumus.

2   Et circa hoc sciendum est quod hoc vocabulum per solius artis respectum inventum est, videlicet ut in quo tota cantionis ars esset contenta, illud diceretur stantia, hoc est mansio capax sive receptaculum totius artis. Nam quemadmodum cantio est gremium totius sententie, sic stantia totam artem ingremiat; nec licet aliquid artis sequentibus arrogare, sed solam artem antecedentis induere. Per quod patet quod ipsa

3   de qua loquimur erit congremiatio sive compages omnium eorum que cantio sumit ab arte: quibus divaricatis, quam querimus descriptio innotescet.

4   Tota igitur scilicet ars cantionis circa tria videtur consistere: primo circa cantus divisionem, secundo circa partium habitudinem, tertio

5   circa numerum carminum et sillabarum. De rithimo vero mentionem non facimus, quia de propria cantionis arte non est. Licet enim in qua-

only with poems in the vernacular, and am not discussing those in the regulated language, I say that there is one form of vernacular poetry that excels all others, and that, on account of its pre-eminence, we call the *canzone*; and that the *canzone* is pre- eminent was proved in the third chapter of this book. And because what has just been defined seems to be common to the majority of instances, I shall now take up afresh what has been defined generically, and identify more precisely, through a series of distinctions, what it is we are seeking, and that alone. So I say that the 8 *canzone*, in so far as it is so called for its pre-eminence, which is what we too are seeking, is a connected series of equal stanzas in the tragic style, without a refrain, and focused on a single theme, as I showed when I wrote

Donne ch'avete intelletto d'amore.[146]

If I say 'a connected series in the tragic style', it is because, were the style of the stanzas comic, we would use the diminutive and call it a *canzonetta*, a form I intend to discuss in the fourth book of the present work.

And now it is clear what a *canzone* is, whether we are using the term 9 in a general sense or on account of the form's outstanding excellence. It seems plain enough what we mean when we call something a *canzone*, and, in consequence, what this bundle we are preparing to tie together may be.

IX

Since, as I have said, a *canzone* is a connected series of stanzas, those 1 who do not know what a stanza is must also fail to understand a *canzone*, for the understanding of a thing that requires definition flows from familiarity with the elements that compose it; and so, in consequence, I must now discuss the stanza, by enquiring exactly what it may be and just what we mean when we use the term.

And about this you must know that this word was coined solely for 2 the purpose of discussing poetic technique, so that the object in which the whole art of the *canzone* was enshrined should be called a stanza, that is, a capacious storehouse or receptacle for the art in its entirety. For just as the *canzone* is the lap of the whole of its subject-matter, so the stanza enlaps its whole technique; and the later stanzas of the poem should never aspire to add any new technical device, but should only dress themselves in the same garb as the first. So it will be clear that that 3 of which we speak will be the enlapment[147] or frame of all the technical

libet stantia rithimos innovare et eosdem reiterare ad libitum: quod, si de propria cantionis arte rithimus esset, minime liceret quod dictum est. Si quid autem rithimi servare interest huius quod est ars, illud comprehenditur ibi cum dicimus 'partium habitudinem'.

6 Quare sic colligere possumus ex predictis diffinientes et dicere stantiam esse sub certo cantu et habitudine limitata carminum et sillabarum compagem.

X

1 Scientes quia rationale animal homo est et quia sensibilis anima et corpus est animal, et ignorantes de hac anima quid ea sit, vel de ipso corpore, perfectam hominis cognitionem habere non possumus: quia cognitionis perfectio uniuscuiusque terminatur ad ultima elementa, sicut Magister Sapientum in principio Physicorum testatur. Igitur ad habendam cantionis cognitionem quam inhyamus, nunc diffinentia suum diffiniens sub compendio ventilemus, et primo de cantu, deinde de habitudine, et postmodum de carminibus et sillabis percontemur.

2 Dicimus ergo quod omnis stantia ad quandam odam recipiendam armonizata est. Sed in modis diversificari videntur. Quia quedam sunt sub una oda continua usque ad ultimum progressive, hoc est sine iteratione modulationis cuiusquam et sine diesi – et diesim dicimus deductionem vergentem de una oda in aliam (hanc voltam vocamus, cum vulgus alloquimur) –: et huiusmodi stantia usus est fere in omnibus cantionibus suis Arnaldus Danielis, et nos eum secuti sumus cum diximus

Al poco giorno e al gran cerchio d'ombra.

3 Quedam vero sunt diesim patientes: et diesis esse non potest, secundum quod eam appellamus, nisi reiteratio unius ode fiat, vel ante

4 diesim, vel post, vel undique. Si ante diesim repetitio fiat, stantiam dicimus habere pedes; et duos habere decet, licet quandoque tres fiant, rarissime tamen. Si repetitio fiat post diesim, tunc dicimus stantiam habere versus. Si ante non fiat repetitio, stantiam dicimus habere frontem. Si post non fiat, dicimus habere sirma, sive caudam.

principles on which the *canzone* draws; and, when we have defined
these, the description we seek will stand out clearly.

The whole technique of the *canzone*, then, is plainly based on these 4
three principles: first, the articulation of the melody, second, the organi-
sation of the parts, and third, the number of lines and syllables. I make no 5
mention of rhyme here, because it is not exclusive to the technique of the
canzone. For it is permissible to introduce new rhymes into any stanza, or
to repeat those already used, according to choice; which, if rhyme be-
longed only to *canzone* technique, would scarcely be allowable – as I have
said. If there are aspects of the use of rhyme that are relevant to the tech-
nique under discussion, they will be included when I discuss the organi-
sation of parts.

So from all that has now been said we can assemble the elements of a de- 6
finition, and say that a stanza is a coherent arrangement of lines and
syllables governed by a particular melody and a clearly defined organis-
ation.

X

If we know that a human being is a rational animal, and that an 1
animal consists of a body and a sensitive soul, but do not know what that
soul is, nor yet that body, we cannot have a perfect understanding of the
human being; for the perfect understanding of anything must take into
account its basic elements, as the master of those who know affirms at
the beginning of his *Physics*.[148] Therefore, in order to acquire that under-
standing of the *canzone* at which we aim, let us now briefly undertake the
definition of the things that define the *canzone* itself, beginning with its
melody, moving on to its organisation, and finally discussing its lines and
syllables.

I say, then, that every stanza is constructed harmoniously for the 2
purpose of having a particular melody attached to it. But it is clear that
stanzas differ in form. For some are accompanied by an uninterrupted
melody, in an ordered progression from beginning to end – that is,
without any repetition of musical phrases or any diesis (and by diesis I
mean a movement from one melody to another, which we call a 'turn'
when speaking the vernacular). Stanzas of this kind were used by Arnaut
Daniel in nearly all his *canzoni*, and I followed him when I wrote

Al poco giorno e al gran cerchio d'ombra.[149]

Some stanzas, on the other hand, tolerate diesis: but there can be no 3
diesis, in the sense in which I use the term, unless one melody be re-

5 Vide ergo, lector, quanta licentia data sit cantiones poetantibus, et considera cuius rei causa tam largum arbitrium usus sibi asciverit; et si recto calle ratio te duxerit, videbis autoritatis dignitate sola quod dicimus esse concessum.

6 Satis hinc innotescere potest quomodo cantionis ars circa cantus divisionem consistat, et ideo ad habitudinem procedamus.

XI

1 Videtur nobis hec quam habitudinem dicimus maxima pars eius quod artis est. Hec etenim circa cantus divisionem atque contextum carminum et rithimorum relationem consistit: quapropter diligentissime videtur esse tractanda.

2 Incipientes igitur dicimus quod frons cum versibus, pedes cum cauda vel sirmate, nec non pedes cum versibus, in stantia se diversimode

3 habere possunt. Nam quandoque frons versus excedit in sillabis et carminibus, vel excedere potest – et dicimus 'potest' quoniam habitudinem

4 hanc adhuc non vidimus. Quandoque in carminibus excedere et in sillabis superari potest, ut si frons esset pentametra et quilibet versus esset dimeter, et metra frontis eptasillaba et versus endecasillaba essent.

5 Quandoque versus frontem superant sillabis et carminibus, ut in illa quam dicimus

Traggemi de la mente amor la stiva:

fuit hec tetrametra frons, tribus endecasillabis et uno eptasillabo contexta; non etenim potuit in pedes dividi, cum equalitas carminum et silla-

6 barum requiratur in pedibus inter se et etiam in versibus inter se. Et quemadmodum dicimus de fronte, dicimus et de versibus: possent etenim versus frontem superare carminibus, et sillabis superari, puta si versus duo essent et uterque trimeter, et eptasillaba metra, et frons esset pentametra, duobus endecasillabis et tribus eptasillabis contexta.

7 Quandoque vero pedes caudam superant carminibus et sillabis, ut in illa quam diximus

peated, either before the diesis, or after it, or on either side. If the repeti- 4
tion occurs before the diesis, we say that the stanza has 'feet' [*pedes*]; and
it should have two of these, although cases do occur – albeit very rarely –
where it has three. If the repetition comes after the diesis, we say that the
stanza has 'verses' [*versus*]. If there is no repetition before the diesis, we
say the stanza has a 'forehead' [*frons*]; if there is none after, then we say it
has a 'tail' [*sirma, cauda*].

So you can see, reader, how much room for manoeuvre is available to 5
those who write *canzoni*, and you should consider why poetic practice
has bestowed such extensive discretionary powers on itself. If reason has
guided you along the right path, you will see that what I describe has
only come about in recognition of the stature of authoritative models.

It should now be clear enough what the technique of the *canzone* has 6
to do with the articulation of the melody; and so let us move on to its orga-
nisation.

XI

In my opinion, what I call organization is the most important aspect, 1
as far as technique is concerned. It depends, in fact, both on the articula-
tion of the melody and on the combination of verses and the relationship
of rhymes: so it must be treated with the greatest care.

To begin with, then, I say that a *frons* with its *versus*, or the *pedes* 2
with their *cauda* or *sirma*, or even *pedes* with *versus*, may have differing re-
lationships with one another within a stanza. For sometimes the *frons* 3
will have more syllables and lines than the *versus*, or at least it can have –
and I say 'can' because I have not yet actually seen a stanza arranged this
way. Sometimes it may have more lines and fewer syllables, as when the 4
frons has five lines and each of the two *versus* only two, but the *frons* is in
heptasyllables and the *versus* in hendecasyllables. Sometimes the *versus* 5
will exceed the *frons* in both number of syllables and number of lines, as
in my *canzone*

Traggemi de la mente amor la stiva:[150]

This had a four-line *frons*, made up of three hendecasyllables and one
heptasyllable; and so it could not be divided into *pedes*, because in the re-
lationship between *pedes* it is necessary that each have an equal number
of lines and syllables, as is also true of *versus*. And what I have already 6
said about the *frons*, I will repeat when speaking of *versus*; for the *versus*
may have more lines and fewer syllables than the *frons*, as when there are

Amor, che movi tua virtù da cielo.

8 Quandoque pedes a sirmate superantur in toto, ut in illa quam diximus

Donna pietosa e di novella etate.

9 Et quemadmodum diximus frontem posse superare carminibus, sillabis superatam (et e converso), sic de sirmate dicimus.

10 Pedes quoque versus in numero superant et superantur ab hiis: possunt enim esse in stantia tres pedes et duo versus, et tres versus et duo pedes; nec hoc numero limitamur, quin liceat plures et pedes et versus

11 simul contexere. Et quemadmodum de victoria carminum et sillabarum diximus inter alia, nunc etiam inter pedes et versus dicimus: nam eodem modo vinci et vincere possunt.

12 Nec pretermictendum est quod nos e contrario regulatis poetis pedes accipimus, quia illi carmen ex pedibus, nos vero ex carminibus pedem

13 constare dicimus, ut satis evidenter apparet. Nec etiam pretermictendum est quin iterum asseramus pedes ab invicem necessario carminum et sillabarum equalitatem et habitudinem accipere, quia non aliter cantus repetitio fieri posset. Hoc idem in versibus esse servandum astruimus.

XII

1 Est etiam, ut superius dictum est, habitudo quedam quam carmina contexendo considerare debemus: et ideo rationem faciamus de illa, repetentes proinde que superius de carminibus diximus.

2 In usu nostro maxime tria carmina frequentandi prerogativam habere videntur, endecasillabum scilicet, eptasillabum et pentasillabum;

3 que trisillabum ante alia sequi astruximus. Horum prorsus, cum tragice poetari conamur, endecasillabum propter quandam excellentiam in contextu vincendi privilegium promeretur. Nam quedam stantia est que solis endecasillabis gaudet esse contexta, ut illa Guidonis de Florentia,

Donna me prega perch'io voglio dire;

et etiam nos dicimus

two *versus*, each of three lines in heptasyllables, and a five-line *frons* woven out of two lines of eleven syllables and three of seven.

Sometimes, moreover, the *pedes* will have more lines and syllables   7 than the *cauda*, as in my poem

Amor, che movi tua virtù da cielo.[151]

Sometimes the *pedes* will be exceeded by the *sirma* as a whole, as in the   8 poem in which I wrote

Donna pietosa e di novella etate.[152]

And just as I have said of the *frons* that it may exceed in lines and be ex-   9 ceeded in syllables (and vice versa), so this is also true of the *sirma*.

Also, the *pedes* may exceed the *versus* in number, or may be exceeded   10 by them; for there may be three *pedes* and two *versus* in a stanza, or indeed three *versus* and two *pedes*. Nor are we bound by these numbers, for it is quite feasible to go on combining *pedes* and *versus* in greater quantities. And what I have already said about the prevalence of lines and syl-   11 lables in the other parts of the stanza's organisation, I now repeat about *pedes* and *versus*: for in the same way each can either gain or yield the upper hand.

Nor should I fail to mention the fact that we use the term 'feet' [*pedes*]   12 in a sense different from that of poets in the regulated language; for they say that a line is made up of feet, whereas for us a foot is made up of lines, as should be clear enough by now. Nor, again, should I fail to reiterate the   13 following point: that in their mutual relationship the *pedes* should be equal, in both number of lines and number of syllables, as well as in their organization; for otherwise it will not be possible to repeat their melody exactly. And I hold that this principle is also to be observed in the *versus*.

XII

As I said above, there is also a principle of organisation to be taken into account when weaving lines together; and so I shall now establish   1 that, bearing in mind everything that was said above about the line itself.

In our usage three kinds of line seem to enjoy the privilege of being   2 employed most often, namely the hendecasyllable, the heptasyllable, and the pentasyllable; and I have pointed out that the trisyllable follows these more closely than the remainder. Of these it is definitely the hendecasyl-   3 lable that earns the highest ranking when we try to write poems in the tragic style, because of its peculiar aptness for such composition. For

Donne ch'avete intelletto d'amore.

Hoc etiam Yspani usi sunt – et dico Yspanos qui poetati sunt in vulgari oc: Namericus de Belnui:

Nuls hom non pot complir adrecciamen.

4 Quedam est in qua tantum eptasillabum intexitur unum: et hoc esse non potest nisi ubi frons est vel cauda, quoniam, ut dictum est, in pedibus atque versibus actenditur equalitas carminum et sillabarum. Propter quod etiam nec numerus impar carminum potest esse ubi frons vel cauda non est; sed ubi hee sunt, vel altera sola, pari et impari numero in 5 carminibus licet uti ad libitum. Et sicut quedam stantia est uno solo eptasillabo conformata, sic duobus, tribus, quatuor, quinque videtur posse 6 contexi, dummodo in tragico vincat endecasillabum et principiet. Verumtamen quosdam ab eptasillabo tragice principiasse invenimus, videlicet Guidonem Guinizelli, Guidonem de Ghisileriis et Fabrutium Bononienses:

Di fermo sofferire,

et

Donna, lo fermo core,

et

Lo meo lontano gire;

et quosdam alios. Sed si ad eorum sensum subtiliter intrare velimus, non sine quodam elegie umbraculo hec tragedia processisse videbitur. 7 De pentasillabo quoque non sic concedimus: in dictamine magno sufficit enim unicum pentasillabum in tota stantia conseri, vel duo ad plus in pedibus – et dico 'pedibus' propter necessitatem qua pedibus, versi- 8 busque, cantatur. Minime autem trisillabum in tragico videtur esse sumendum per se subsistens – et dico 'per se subsistens' quia per quandam rithimorum repercussionem frequenter videtur assumptum, sicut inveniri potest in illa Guidonis Florentini,

Donna me prega,

et in illa quam diximus

Poscia ch'Amor del tutto m'ha lasciato.

Nec per se ibi carmen est omnino, sed pars endecasillabi tantum, ad rithimum precedentis carminis velut econ respondens.
9   Hoc etiam precipue actendendum est circa carminum habitudinem,

there are some stanzas that seem to rejoice in being composed entirely of hendecasyllables, as in that poem of Guido of Florence:

Donna me prega, perch'io voglio dire;[153]

or as I myself wrote:

Donne ch'avete intelletto d'amore.[154]

The Hispanic poets[155] have also used this device: and by Hispanic I mean those who have written poetry in the language of *oc*, such as Aimeric de Belenoi:

Nuls hom non pot complir adrecciamen.[156]

There exists one kind of stanza in which a single heptasyllable is included; but this can only occur where there is a *frons* or a *cauda*, since, as I said, in *pedes* and *versus* the principle of equal numbers of lines and syllables must be strictly observed. For this reason, moreover, there cannot be an odd number of lines where there is no *frons* or *cauda*; but when these are present, or even if only one of them is, you can have odd or even numbers of lines, as you please. And just as there is a kind of stanza that includes only one heptasyllable, so it will be evident that stanzas can be composed that include two, three, four, or five of them, as long as, in the tragic style, it is the hendecasyllable that occupies the place of honour and sets the tone at the outset. It is true that I have seen cases in which a tragic poem has begun with a heptasyllable, as in these examples from Guido Guinizzelli, Guido Ghislieri, and Fabruzzo, all three from Bologna:

Di fermo sofferire,[157]

and

Donna, lo fermo core,[158]

and

Lo meo lontano gire;[159]

and a few others. But if we are willing to analyse the meaning of these examples more subtly, we will find that this is a tragic poetry with more than a hint of the elegiac about it. The same concession, however, cannot be made for the pentasyllable: in a poem in the high style it will be enough if a single pentasyllable be inserted into the whole stanza, or two, at the most, in the *pedes*; and I say 'in the *pedes*' because of the need to maintain equality in the melody of *pedes* and *versus*. The trisyllable should most cer-

quod, si eptasillabum interseratur in primo pede, quem situm accipit ibi, eundem resumat in altero: puta, si pes trimeter primum et ultimum carmen endecasillabum habet et medium, hoc est secundum, eptasillabum, ‹et pes alter habeat secundum eptasillabum› et extrema endecasillaba: non aliter ingeminatio cantus fieri posset, ad quam pedes fiunt, 10 ut dictum est, et per consequens pedes esse non possent. Et quemadmodum de pedibus, dicimus et de versibus: in nullo enim pedes et versus differre videmus nisi in situ, quia hii ante, hii post diesim stantie nominantur. Et etiam quemadmodum de trimetro pede, et de omnibus aliis servandum esse asserimus; et sicut de uno eptasillabo, sic de pluribus et de pentasillabo et omni alio dicimus.

11   Satis hinc, lector, elicere sufficienter potes qualiter tibi carminum habituanda sit stantia habitudinemque circa carmina considerandam videre.

XIII

1   Rithimorum quoque relationi vacemus, nichil de rithimo secundum se modo tractantes: proprium enim eorum tractatum in posterum prorogamus, cum de mediocri poemate intendemus.

2   In principio igitur huius capituli quedam resecanda videntur. Unum est stantia sine rithimo, in qua nulla rithimorum habitudo actenditur: et huiusmodi stantiis usus est Arnaldus Danielis frequentissime, velut ibi:

Se.m fos Amor de ioi donar;

et nos dicimus

tainly not be used standing alone in the tragic style; and I say 'standing alone' because it can often be seen to be used to create an effect of echo between rhymes, as will be found in Guido of Florence's

Donna me prega,[160]

and in my own poem

Poscia ch'Amor del tutto m'ha lasciato.[161]

Here the line has no independent existence at all, but is only a segment of the hendecasyllable, answering the rhyme of the previous line like an echo.

Particular attention needs to be paid to this point where the organisa- 9 tion of the lines is concerned, for, if a heptasyllable is included in the first foot, another must occupy the corresponding position in the second; so that, if a three-line *pes* has hendecasyllables in first and third place and in the middle, as the second line, a heptasyllable, then the other *pes* must also have a heptasyllable in the middle and a hendecasyllable on either side. Otherwise, it will not be possible to repeat the melody exactly, which is the purpose for which the *pedes* are designed, as I said above, and thus they will not really be *pedes*. And what is true of the *pedes*, I say is also true 10 of the *versus*: it will be clear that there is no difference between *pedes* and *versus* but that of position, since the former are so called because they occur before the stanza's diesis, and the latter because they occur after it. Besides, I affirm that the rules laid down for the three-line *pes* are also to be followed for all other *pedes*; and, as for a single heptasyllable, so also for more than one, and so on with the pentasyllable and every other kind of line.

From all this, reader, you should be able to work out easily enough 11 what kinds of line[162] are to be used for composing a stanza and what needs to be taken into account when considering the organisation of the lines themselves.

XIII

Let us now deal with the relationship of rhymes, though without, for 1 the moment, saying anything about rhyme itself; for I have postponed a more detailed treatment of that subject to the section in which I deal with the middle level of poetic style.

It will, therefore, be useful to anticipate some elements of the discus- 2 sion at the beginning of this chapter. One of these is the unrhymed

Al poco giorno.

3   Aliud est stantia cuius omnia carmina eundem rithimum reddunt, in qua superfluum esse constat habitudinem querere. Sic proinde restat circa rithimos mixtos tantum debere insisti.

4   Et primo sciendum est quod in hoc amplissimam sibi licentiam fere omnes assumunt, et ex hoc maxime totius armonie dulcedo intenditur.

5   Sunt etenim quidam qui non omnes quandoque desinentias carminum rithimantur in eadem stantia, sed easdem repetunt sive rithimantur in aliis, sicut fuit Gottus Mantuanus, qui suas multas et bonas cantiones nobis oretenus intimavit: hic semper in stantia unum carmen incomitatum texebat, quod clavem vocabat; et sicut de uno licet, licet etiam de duobus, et forte de pluribus.

6   Quidam alii sunt, et fere omnes cantionum inventores, qui nullum in stantia carmen incomitatum relinquunt quin sibi rithimi concrepan-
7   tiam reddant, vel unius vel plurium. Et quidam diversos faciunt esse rithimos eorum que post diesim carmina sunt a rithimis eorum que sunt ante; quidam vero non sic, sed desinentias anterioris stantie inter postera carmina referentes intexunt. Sepissime tamen hoc fit in desinentia primi posteriorum, quam plerique rithimantur ei que est priorum posterioris: quod non aliud esse videtur quam quedam ipsius stantie concatenatio
8   pulcra. De rithimorum quoque habitudine, prout sunt in fronte vel in cauda, videtur omnis optata licentia concedenda; pulcerrime tamen se habent ultimorum carminum desinentie si cum rithimo in silentium cadant.

9   In pedibus vero cavendum est: et habitudinem quandam servatam esse invenimus. Et, discretionem facientes, dicimus quod pes vel pari vel impari metro completur, et utrobique comitata et incomitata desinentia esse potest: nam in pari metro nemo dubitat; in alio vero, si quis dubius est, recordetur ea que diximus in preinmediato capitulo de trisillabo,
10   quando, pars existens endecasillabi, velut econ respondet. Et si in altero pedum exsortem rithimi desinentiam esse contingat, omnimode in altero sibi instauratio fiat. Si vero quelibet desinentia in altero pede rithimi consortium habeat, in altero prout libet referre vel innovare desinentias licet, vel totaliter vel in parte, dumtaxat precedentium ordo servetur in totum: puta, si extreme desinentie trimetri, hoc est prima et ultima, concrepabunt in primo pede, sic secundi extremas desinentias convenit concrepare; et qualem se in primo media videt, comitatam quidem vel incomitatam, talis in secundo resurgat: et sic de aliis pedibus
11   est servandum. In versibus quoque fere semper hac lege perfruimur – et 'fere' dicimus quia propter concatenationem prenotatam et combina-

stanza, in which no organisation according to rhyme occurs; Arnaut Daniel used this kind of stanza very frequently, as in his

Se.m fos Amor de ioi donar;[163]

and I also used it in

Al poco giorno.[164]

Another is the stanza in which every line ends with the same rhyme, 3 and in this case it would obviously be superfluous to enquire further into the stanza's organisation. So all that remains is the obligation to pursue the analysis of stanzas with more than one rhyme.

First of all you must know that almost all poets grant themselves a 4 considerable degree of licence in this matter, and this is mostly what they aim at to achieve the sweetness of the overall harmony. There are some, 5 indeed, who do not always rhyme all the endings within a single stanza, but repeat them or rhyme them in later stanzas. One who did this was Gotto of Mantua, who recited many of his excellent *canzoni* to me in person; he always wove one line with no matching rhyme into every stanza, and called it the key-line.[165] And what can be done with one line can also be done with two, and perhaps with more.

There are certain others, perhaps the large majority of writers of 6 *canzoni*, who avoid leaving any line in a stanza unaccompanied, but always provide it with the accord offered by rhyme, whether in one line or several. And some make the rhymes in the lines that come after the 7 diesis differ from those in the lines that come before it, while others do not do this, but instead carry the endings from the first part of the stanza forward, and weave them into the later lines. This is most often done, however, with the ending of the first line of the latter portion of the stanza, which the majority of writers rhyme with the last line of the earlier portion; and thus they achieve what is clearly none other than a beautiful linking together of the stanza as a whole. As for the organisa- 8 tion of rhymes, in so far as they are used in the *frons* or the *cauda* it seems that as much liberty as may be desired must be allowed; but the effect will be particularly beautiful if the endings of the last lines cause the stanza to fall silent on a rhyme.

In the *pedes*, however, some caution is required; for here we find that 9 some rules of organisation are to be observed. And, making a distinction, I say that a *pes* may be made up of an even or an odd number of lines, and that in either case its endings may or may not be matched with rhymes. No one will doubt that this is true for an even number of lines; but if anyone doubts that it is also true in the opposite case, let him recall what

tionem desinentiarum ultimarum quandoque ordinem iam dictum perverti contingit.

12   Preterea nobis bene convenire videtur ut que cavenda sunt circa rithimos huic appendamus capitulo, cum in isto libro nichil ulterius de
13   rithimorum doctrina tangere intendamus. Tria ergo sunt que circa rithimorum positionem potiri dedecet aulice poetantem: nimia scilicet eiusdem rithimi repercussio, nisi forte novum aliquid atque intentatum artis hoc sibi preroget – ut nascentis militie dies, qui cum nulla prerogativa suam indignatur preterire dietam: hoc etenim nos facere nisi sumus ibi:

Amor, tu vedi ben che questa donna;

secundum vero est ipsa inutilis equivocatio, que semper sententie quicquam derogare videtur; et tertium est rithimorum asperitas, nisi forte sit lenitati permixta: nam lenium asperorumque rithimorum mixtura ipsa tragedia nitescit.

14   Et hec de arte, prout habitudinem respicit, tanta sufficiant.

XIV

1   Ex quo ‹duo› que sunt artis in cantione satis sufficienter tractavimus, nunc de tertio videtur esse tractandum, videlicet de numero carminum et sillabarum. Et primo secundum totam stantiam videre oportet aliquid; deinde secundum partes eius videbimus.

2   Nostra igitur primo refert discretionem facere inter ea que canenda occurrunt, quia quedam stantie prolixitatem videntur appetere, quedam

I said in the immediately preceding chapter about the trisyllable, when, as part of a hendecasyllable, it answers like an echo. And if there 10 should be an ending lacking a rhyme in the first foot, a matching rhyme should at all costs be provided for it in the second. If, however, every ending in one foot has its matching rhyme, in the other you may repeat the endings or introduce new ones, as you please, either completely or partially, as long as the order of the foregoing rhymes is maintained throughout. Thus, if the outside endings of a three-line *pes*, that is, those of the first and third lines, are matched with each other, then the equivalent endings in the second *pes* must also match; and however the middle line of the first is treated, whether provided with a rhyme or not, it must re-appear likewise in the second – and the same scheme must be followed in any other type of *pes*. Finally, the same rule is almost always 11 followed in the *versus*; though I say 'álmost' because, owing to the linking together mentioned above, and to the matching of the final line-endings, the order that I have described is sometimes found to be sub-verted.

Besides all this, it seems to me most appropriate to add to this 12 chapter a note on what to beware of when using rhyme, since I do not intend to return to the theory of rhyme as a subject anywhere in the present book.[166] There are, then, three ways of placing rhymes that are 13 inappropriate for a poet in the high style: one is hammering on the same rhyme, unless perhaps he thereby claims for himself something new and previously unattempted in the art; then the poet is like a knight on the day of his dubbing, who scorns to let it pass without some special exploit. This is what I tried to do here:

Amor, tu vedi ben che questa donna;[167]

The second thing to avoid is that superfluous kind of rhyme called 'equi-vocal', which always seems to detract to some extent from meaning; and the third is the use of harsh-sounding rhymes, unless they be mixed with gentle-sounding ones – for in fact it is the mingling of harsh and gentle rhymes that gives tragedy its splendour.

And let this be enough about technique, as far as it concerns the orga- 14 nization of the stanza.

XIV

Since I have now treated two aspects of *canzone* technique in sufficient 1 depth, it is clearly time to discuss a third, namely the number of lines and

non. Nam cum ea que dicimus cuncta vel circa dextrum aliquid vel sinistrum canamus – ut quandoque persuasorie quandoque dissuasorie, quandoque gratulanter quandoque yronice, quandoque laudabiliter quandoque contemptive canere contingit –, que circa sinistra sunt verba semper ad extremum festinent, et alia decenti prolixitate passim veniant ad extremum...

syllables. And first of all we must consider the matter from the point of view of the whole stanza; after which we will go on to look at its separate parts.

First of all, then, I must draw a distinction among the subjects that 2 lend themselves to poetry, for some of them seem to require a stanza of a certain length, while others do not. For since everything we touch upon in poetry can be treated either positively or negatively[168] – so that sometimes we sing to persuade and sometimes to dissuade, or sometimes sincerely and sometimes ironically, or sometimes to praise and sometimes to scorn – so the words that treat subjects negatively should always hasten to make an end, while the others should always reach their destination at an agreeably measured pace...

Explanatory notes

1 Literally, 'grammar'; in Dante's usage (also attested in the *Convivio*), it normally means merely 'Latin', but in the lexicon of the *De vulgari eloquentia* it is consistently used to mean 'a literary language governed by rules', identifiable, at most, with Latin *as written by the best poets* (the 'regulati poetae' – see n. 108 below). For this reason I have avoided translating it simply as 'Latin', since so many kinds of actual Latin (prose, the spoken language, etc.) are excluded from *gramatica* in Dante's rigorous theoretical conception.

2 Here, as elsewhere in the treatise, the basic axioms of Dante's thinking and argument are derived from Aristotle by way of the tradition of late medieval Christian scholasticism. On this intellectual heritage in general, see the classic work of Kenelm Foster, *The Two Dantes and Other Studies* (London, 1977).

3 For the serpent, see Genesis 3. 1–5; for Balaam's ass, Numbers 22. 28–30.

4 *Metamorphoses*, v. 294–9.

5 'magpie'.

6 Mengaldo's 1968 edition reads 'locutionem' ('speech') for Marigo's 'speculationem', but in 1979 he reverted without comment to the older reading. In the light of the discussion of angelic communication in I. ii. 3–4 above, 'speculationem' seems clearly preferable.

7 Marigo (p. 18) reads 'obtentus', 'covered over', for 'obtectus'.

8 See I. i. 2 above ('Sed quia unamquanque doctrinam oportet non probare, sed suum aperire subiectum. . .').

9 Genesis 3. 2–3.

10 On Dante's somewhat idiosyncratic view of this question, see Dino Castaldo, 'L'etica del *primoloquium* di Adamo nel *De vulgari eloquentia*', *Italica*, 59 (1982): pp. 3–15.

11 This image, familiar to English-speaking readers from Shakespeare's *King Lear* ('When we are born, we cry that we are come / to this great stage of fools'), has its roots in the apocryphal Book of Wisdom (7. 3), and is also found in Pliny's *Natural History* (7, proem), and many medieval texts.

12 In I. ii. 3–4 above, Dante had argued that the angels have no need of speech; but if they do not, neither, clearly, does their creator, God. Hence the qualifications that follow, making clear that God 'speaks' to human beings by choice and not necessity, and in a fashion wholly His own.

13 There is some dispute among scholars as to what is meant here by 'superioribus' and 'inferioribus' – is it 'higher and lower kinds of knowledge' (perhaps theology and natural philosophy, as Marigo suggests, or Giambattista Giuliani's idea of divine authority and human reasoning, expressed in his commentary on this passage in *Opere latine di Dante Alighieri* [Florence, 1878]), or is it simply 'mentioned above in this work and to be returned to below', as Mengaldo (1979, p. 46n.) insists? Though the latter seems to be the meaning of the usage in I. xii. 9, the terms are used figuratively to mean 'better' and 'worse' in II. i. 3, II. i. 10, and II. iv. 5; accordingly, I have chosen here to translate rather than interpret the Latin.

14 The late medieval consensus, stemming from interpretation of Genesis 2. 15, was that the creation of Adam took place outside Paradise; but the question was still controversial.

15 Adam, who was neither born nor grew up in the usual human way.

16 A village on the road from Florence to Bologna, apparently proverbial as a small town with delusions of grandeur.

17 This, of course, is one clue that helps to date the *De vulgari eloquentia*, since it places the composition of this passage after Dante's condemnation to exile in January 1302.

18 This derivation, based on Genesis 10. 24–5 and 11. 14–17, is a commonplace in Augustine's *City of God* (c. 413–26), Isidore of Seville's seventh-century *Etymologies*, and several other highly influential works that were probably on Dante's reference shelf throughout his career.

19 As mentioned in the Introduction, a different account is given, by Adam himself, in *Paradiso* XXVI.

20 The feminine substantive *nequitatrix* (from Late Latin *nequitare* 'to do evil'), applied here to human nature, appears to be a Dantean coinage.

21 The reference is, of course, to the story of the Flood and Noah's Ark (Genesis 6–8).

22 This expression would seem to be roughly equivalent to the modern American saying, 'the third time works the charm'.

23 For the biblical version of Babel, see Genesis 11. 1–9. The idea that Nimrod [Nembroth] was the instigator of this audacious enterprise – which is not justified by the text of Genesis – goes back at least to Augustine, *City of God*, XVI. 4. On Dante's Nimrod, both here and especially in the *Comedy*, see chapter 2 ('The Giants in Hell') of Peter Dronke, *Dante and Medieval Latin Traditions* (Cambridge, 1986), pp. 32–54.

24 i.e., Asia Minor, as subject to the Byzantine Empire.

25 i.e., the *confusio linguarum* inflicted on the builders of the Tower of Babel, described above.

26 The marshes of the Danube estuary are so called by Orosius, Isidore, and many later medieval authors.

27 i.e., the boundaries of those nations with the lands to their north, not with each other.

28 i.e., speakers of Provençal and Catalan.

29 Marigo (pp. 57–8) reads 'a septentrione et occidente anglico sive gallico mari' ('on the north and west . . . by the English or French sea').

30 Marigo (p. 62) reads 'quod prius probatum est', 'which has already been proved'.

31 Giraut de Borneil (c. 1140–c. 1200). For this poem, see Ruth Verity Sharman, *The Cansos and Sirventes of the Troubadour Giraut de Borneil: A Critical Edition* (Cambridge, 1989), pp. 181–6. Sharman's translation of the quoted lines reads 'If I felt I were a genuine and accepted lover, I would indeed bring charges against love' (p. 184).

32 Thibaut de Champagne, King of Navarre, is the only *trouvère*, or lyric poet in *langue d'oïl*, named by Dante. This fact, along with the incorrect attribution to him of *Ire d'amor que en mon cor repaire* (see n. 128 below), and the (greater than usual) textual uncertainty of Dante's citations, has led many scholars to conclude that Dante knew much less about this literature than about its *langue d'oc* counterpart. For the poem beginning with this line (which means 'From true love come knowledge and goodness'), see *Les chansons de Thibaut de Champagne, roi de Navarre*, edited by A. Wallensköld (Paris, 1925), pp. 16–19. Wallensköld reads 'bone' ('good') for Dante's 'fin'.

33 Guido Guinizzelli (c. 1240–c. 1276) was apparently revered as their most significant predecessor by Dante and the other poets (including Guido Cavalcanti and Cino da Pistoia, both quoted in the *De vulgari eloquentia*) usually associated with the innovative poetic style of the 1290s known as the *dolce stil novo*. Dante here quotes lines 3–4 ('Nor did nature create love before the gentle heart, nor the gentle heart before love') of Guinizzelli's *Al cor gentil rempaira sempre amore*; see *Poeti del Duecento*, edited by Gianfranco Contini, 2 vols. (Milan and Naples, 1960), II, pp. 460–4. For an English version with commentary, see *The Poetry of Guido Guinizelli*, edited and translated by Robert Edwards (New York and London, 1987), pp. 20–5 and 108–16.

34 Marigo (p. 66) reads 'principaliter' ('principally'); I follow Mengaldo in reading 'principalius', as an adjective.

35 Dante's Latin refers to the 'right-hand' and 'left-hand' sides of Italy (*dextre Ytalie . . . sinistre*), taking the perspective – traditional in medieval cartography – of an imaginary observer standing on the Alps and looking south. See also I. x. 46, below.

36 It is not clear why Pavia is chosen as an example at this point: ingenious conjectures have been proposed (that the *De vulgari eloquentia* was written there, for instance, or that the use of 'Papienses' is a punning tribute to the eleventh-century lexicographer Papias), but none has been generally accepted. Mengaldo (1979) suggests, plausibly enough, that 'la scelta . . . può essere benissimo casuale' (p. 77 n. 3).

37 The reference seems to be to universal histories of the kind, popular in the

Middle Ages, that began with the Creation and went on to integrate historical material from the Bible with classical material, sometimes coming relatively close to contemporary times.

38 It is not known exactly how widely Dante read in the (vast) medieval Arthurian tradition; but, since the reference here is clearly to works in prose, and given the background of more specific Arthurian allusions elsewhere in his writings (most notoriously in Francesca's sugared apologia in *Inferno* V), the French prose *Lancelot* and perhaps the *Mort le roi Artu* are certainly among the most plausible candidates.

39 Peire d'Alvernha (fl. 1149–68) is the only troubadour named but not quoted in the *De vulgari eloquentia*, which makes it difficult to assess the nature or basis of Dante's admiration for his work.

40 Cino da Pistoia (*c.* 1270–*c.* 1336) lyric poet, practitioner of the *dolce stil novo*, and friend and correspondent of Dante; 'his friend' is plainly Dante himself.

41 Marigo (p. 80) reads 'fictile culmen', 'the clay ridge [of a tiled roof]').

42 *De bello civili* [*Pharsalia*], II. 394–438.

43 i.e., of Spoleto.

44 'Sir, what do you say?'

45 Scholars are not agreed on this phrase's meaning; 'be as you are' seems reasonable, but does not solve the puzzle presented by 'chignamente'.

46 'I met a woman from Fermo near Cascioli; she hurried briskly away, in great haste.' For full text and commentary, see Contini, I, pp. 913–18.

47 'Around the hour of vespers, it was in the month of October'.

48 'What are you up to?'

49 'My house', 'my master'; both are unadulterated Latin. Marigo (p. 94) reads 'dominus nova' and 'domus novus'; but his explanatory note (pp. 95–6) is not altogether convincing. The point of this sentence's comparison of Sardinians to apes is that apes imitate humans *accurately*; but Marigo's proposed readings are, of course, *inaccurate* Latin.

50 'Although water flees from fire'; by Guido delle Colonne (*c.* 1210–*c.* 1287), a leading figure in the group of early thirteenth-century lyric poets known as the *scuola siciliana* or Sicilian school: see Contini, I, pp. 107–10. For English versions and commentary, see *The Poetry of the Sicilian School*, edited and translated by Frede Jensen (New York and London, 1986).

51 'Love, who long have led me'; also by Guido delle Colonne. See Contini, I, pp. 104–6.

52 Sicily; the epithet (derived from Greek, it means 'having three promontories') is common in Virgil.

53 The Emperor Frederick II (1194–1250) was the patron of the *scuola siciliana* poets, whose activity seems to have come to an end with his death. His illegitimate son Manfred (*c.* 1232–66) succeeded him and continued his bitter rivalry with the papacy, but was killed at the battle of Benevento. He appears as a character, saved from damnation by the skin of his teeth,

in *Purgatorio* III. Frederick, however, is mentioned in *Inferno* x as having been damned as a heretic.

54 Marigo (p. 99) and Mengaldo (1979, p. 101) both render 'gratiarum' as 'doni divini', but it may be that, as the plural form suggests, Dante here means courtly graces rather than divine grace.

55 Indeed, it has not done so yet – *scuola siciliana* is still the conventional term in Italian literary historiography.

56 'Thou fool'; compare Matthew 5. 22.

57 Dante refers here to Frederick II of Aragon, king of Sicily from 1296 to 1337, and the Emperor Frederick II's grandson (by Manfred's daughter Costanza); Charles II of Anjou, Frederick's rival for the throne of Naples; Giovanni I, marquis of Monferrato from 1292 to 1305; and Azzo VIII, marquis of Este from 1293 to 1308. All were deeply involved in the internecine warfare that racked Italy at the turn of the thirteenth and fourteenth centuries, and all are mentioned disparagingly elsewhere in Dante's writings, most notably in *Purgatorio* VII.

58 'Get me out of this fire, if you would be so kind'; line 3 of the so-called *Contrasto* of the Sicilian poet Cielo d'Alcamo (fl. 1230–50): see Contini, I, pp. 173–85.

59 'I would like the boy to cry.'

60 'Lady, I wish to tell you'; by Giacomo da Lentini (fl. 1230–40), usually considered both the 'founder' of the *scuola siciliana* and the 'inventor' of the sonnet: see Contini, I, pp. 49–54.

61 'I go so happily for true love's sake'; by Rinaldo d'Aquino (fl. c. 1240), another poet associated with the *scuola siciliana* (although his toponymic seems to indicate that he came from the mainland): see Contini, I, pp. 112–14 (reading 'allegramente' for Dante's 'letamente').

62 Guittone d'Arezzo (c. 1230–94), poet of the generation preceding Dante's own, and the single author towards whom Dante seems to have felt the most acute 'anxiety of influence': see Contini, I, pp. 189–255.

63 Bonagiunta Orbicciani da Lucca (c. 1230–before 1300), poet and rival of Guinizzelli, who appears as a character in *Purgatorio* XXIV, and there pays tribute to Dante and his fellow-practitioners of the *dolce stil novo*: see Contini, I, pp. 257–82.

64 Mid thirteenth-century lyric poet, called 'Galletto' in surviving manuscripts; see Contini, I, pp. 283–8.

65 Thirteenth-century lyric poet, usually known as Bartolomeo Mocati.

66 Brunetto Latini (c. 1220–c. 1295), poet and scholar, probably at some stage Dante's mentor, and controversially immortalised as the protagonist of *Inferno* XV.

67 'Let's eat, since there's nothing else to do.'

68 'The business at Florence went well for Pisa.'

69 'I swear to God, the city of Lucca is really in the pink.'

70 'If only I'd left Siena for good! What's up now?'

71 'Do you want to go somewhere?'
72 Guido Cavalcanti (c. 1255–1300), Lapo Gianni (fl. 1290–1310), Dante himself ('one other'), and Cino da Pistoia are usually seen as the leading figures connected with the *dolce stil novo* – which, on the basis of a much-discussed passage in *Purgatorio* xxiv, is thought to have aimed at the stylistic revivification of lyric poetry in Italian at the end of the thirteenth century. The nature of the 'consideration that is far from unworthy' remains debatable.
73 'God, yes!'
74 'My eye'.
75 'My heart'.
76 Mid thirteenth-century poets. For Tommaso's few surviving poems, see G. Zaccagnini's edition in *Archivum romanicum*, 19 (1935), pp. 79–106; for those of Ugolino del Buzzuola, see Ferdinando Torraca, *Studi danteschi* (Naples, 1912), 187–211.
77 'If only'.
78 'Traded'.
79 'Goodness'.
80 'Nine'.
81 'Alive'.
82 'By God's wounds, you won't come.' According to Marigo (pp. 121–2n.), this is the first line of a well-known Venetian popular song. It is an *endecasillabo tronco* (eleven-syllable line with stress on the last syllable), which Dante would have seen as inferior to the *endecasillabo piano* (stressed on the penultimate syllable) used in serious poetry – see the discussion in ii. v and ii. xi–xii, below.
83 Aldobrandino dei Mezzabati (fl. 1290–1300), who was involved in Florentine politics in 1291–92 as well as writing poetry.
84 Sordello (c. 1220–1269) wrote his (impressive) poetry in *langue d'oc*, hence this remark; he is a major character in *Purgatorio* vi–ix.
85 'Very'.
86 Information about all these mid thirteenth-century poets can be found in *Le rime dei poeti bolognesi del secolo XIII*, edited by Tommaso Casini, second edition (Bologna, 1968); but the poems by Ghislieri, Fabruzzo and Onesto that Dante quotes have not survived.
87 'Lady, the true love that I bear you'; see Contini, ii, pp. 453–6; Edwards, pp. 6–13 and 93–102.
88 'Lady, the faithful heart'.
89 'My distant wandering'.
90 'No longer do I expect your help, love'.
91 The basic source for this doctrine, a scholastic commonplace, is Aristotle, *Metaphysics*, x. 1.
92 Marigo (p. 140) reads 'in bruto animali' ('in brute beasts') after 'magis redolet quam', and then repeats the phrase in square brackets as an

alleged scribal omission before 'quam in planta'; in this he follows the Berlin manuscript's omission of 'in' between 'bruto' and 'animali', while Mengaldo prefers, for once, the reading of the other two surviving manuscripts, *G* and *T*.

93 In the chiasmic structure of this sentence, the philosopher Seneca represents great teachers ('excellenter magistrati excellenter magistrent'), Numa Pompilius, traditionally the second king of Rome, just rulers ('potestate illuminati'). Seneca was relatively well known in the late Middle Ages, especially from the twelfth century onwards, and appears as one of the virtuous pagans in *Inferno* IV; Numa Pompilius was known to Dante from his reading of Livy (who, according to *Inferno* XXVIII. 12, 'non erra').

94 Marigo (p. 148) reads 'vocemus' ('we call') for Mengaldo's 'vocetur' ('is called'). The translation is not affected.

95 'Aula' and 'curia' could both be translated 'court'; but 'aula' implies 'royal court' and 'curia', 'law-court'. To minimise the potential for confusion, I have avoided 'court' and its cognates altogether when rendering 'curia'.

96 This king appears to be Albert of Austria, crowned King of the Romans and hence leading candidate for the imperial throne in 1298, and the 'Alberto tedesco' so scathingly rebuked in *Purgatorio* VI.

97 Marigo (p. 156) reads 'aulicum esse et curiale', which seems to add nothing to the sense, and indeed is ignored in Marigo's own translation (p. 157).

98 Not all these 'following books', of course, exist; see the Introduction, pp. xiv–xv, on the unfinished state of the *De vulgari eloquentia*. For other references in the text to Dante's apparent intentions, see II. iv. 1, II. iv. 6, and II. viii. 8.

99 One of the basic images of poetic composition in Book Two of the *De vulgari eloquentia* is that of 'binding together' the separate elements that make up a poem, especially a canzone. The rare words *avieo, -ere* ('to bind') and *avientes* ('binders'), known to Dante from Isidore of Seville and his twelfth-century epigone Uguccione da Pisa, are thus used here as the metaphorical equivalents of 'writing poetry' and 'poets'. In the *Convivio* (IV. vi. 34), Dante explains that the vernacular word *autore* derives in part from *avieo*, and is therefore used 'solo per li poeti, che con l'arte musaica le loro parole hanno legate'.

100 Another bold metaphor: *carminare* literally means 'to card wool', so here it has the sense of clarifying or untangling a complex problem, making appropriate distinctions, and revealing its underlying basis. Significantly for Dante, no doubt, Isidore and Uguccione both connect the word, etymologically, with *carmina facere* ('to make songs').

101 Each of these examples is related to a different one of the categories listed in the first half of the sentence: because all animals have sense-perceptions, human beings have them in respect of their (animal) genus; because human beings alone have the power to laugh, they have it in respect of

their (human) species; and when a human being rides, or performs any other action, he or she does so in respect of him- or herself – i.e., as an individual. The (Aristotelian) idea that laughter, like speech, is unique to human beings is also found in Dante's *Vita nuova*, xxv. 2: 'Dico anche di lui che ridea, e anche che parlava; le quali cose paiono essere proprie de l'uomo.'

102 'I cannot refrain from sending forth my song'; see Gérard Gouiran, *L'amour et la guerre: l'œuvre de Bertran de Born*, 2 vols. (Aix-en-Provence and Marseille, 1985), II, pp. 569–92. Bertran de Born (*c*. 1140–1215) had a political as well as a poetic career, the vicissitudes of which earned him a place among the sowers of discord in *Inferno* xxvIII.

103 'The bitter breeze / makes the leafy copses / whiten': see *The Poetry of Arnaut Daniel*, edited and translated by James J. Wilhelm (New York and London, 1981), pp. 34–9. Arnaut (fl. *c*. 1175–*c*. 1200) seems to have been the troubadour poet most admired by Dante, as suggested both by the several quotations in the *De vulgari eloquentia* and by his presence – speaking *langue d'oc* – in *Purgatorio* xxvi.

104 Sharman (pp. 467–73) translates 'To re-awaken the joys of company / which have sunk into too sound a sleep' (p. 470).

105 'I am worthy of death'; see Contini, II, pp. 635–6.

106 'Grief brings boldness to my heart'; see *Dante's Lyric Poetry*, edited and translated by Kenelm Foster and Patrick Boyde, 2 vols. (Oxford, 1967), I, pp. 182–92 and II, pp. 295–310.

107 Marigo (p. 182) reads 'pensamus', with manuscripts *G* and *T*; the translation is not affected.

108 Here and throughout Book Two, 'the rules' are those of Latin, and the poets who follow them (the 'regular' poets) are those of the classical Latin tradition. Significantly, however, and in keeping with its consistent avoidance of this terminology, the text of the *De vulgari eloquentia* never uses any designation that would identify them as such.

109 *Ars poetica*, 38.

110 In Greco-Roman mythology, a mountain beloved of the Muses, whose streams gave inspiration to those who drank from them.

111 The allusion, on which the following sentence elaborates, is to the famous Virgilian tag, *Aeneid*, vI. 129.

112 *Aeneid*, vI. 126–31. Ernst Robert Curtius, *European Literature and the Latin Middle Ages*, translated by Willard R. Trask (London, 1953), suggests (p. 359) that Dante took this interpretation from the twelfth-century commentary on the *Aeneid* by Bernardus Silvestris; Mengaldo (1979, p. 168n.), inclines to agree. Giorgio Padoan, in his entry on Bernardus in the *Enciclopedia dantesca* (Rome, 1970–8), I, pp. 606–7, is more circumspect about the direct filiation from Bernardus to Dante. See also Theodore Silverstein, 'Dante and Vergil the Mystic', *Harvard Studies and Notes in Philology and Literature*, 14 (1932), pp. 51–82; and, for the text of Bernardus's commentary, *Com-*

mentum quod dicitur Bernardi Silvestris super sex libros Eneidos Virgilii, edited by Julian and Elizabeth Jones (Lincoln, USA, 1977).

113 The adjective *astripetus* (*astra* 'the stars' + *petere,* 'to seek') appears to be Dante's own coinage.

114 i.e., Giraut de Borneil; Sharman (pp. 71–6) translates 'Now you shall hear first-class songs' (p. 74).

115 See above, n. 32.

116 At first sight this line appears to contain only ten syllables, one short of the number required for a hendecasyllable. Dante seems, by his somewhat obscure phrasing here, to be suggesting that *bontè,* deriving as it does from forms with penultimate rather than final stress (*bonitate, bonitade*), retains that arrangement even when the stressed vowel in the next-to-last syllable has become fused, in pronunciation, with the unstressed vowel in the last (*bonitate*-bontáe-*bontè*). The line thus has eleven syllables, the last counting for metrical purposes, as it were, as two. See Marigo (p. 200n.).

117 See above, n. 33.

118 See above, n. 51.

119 See above, n. 61.

120 'I have no hope that ever for my benefit'; see *Poeti del dolce stil nuovo,* edited by Mario Marti (Florence, 1969), pp. 505–8.

121 'Love, who send your power down from heaven'; see Foster and Boyde, I, pp. 117–22 and II, pp. 192–9.

122 The Latin of this sentence is 'flavourless' because it fails to observe the conventions of writing prose based on the rhythmic schemes known as *cursus.* In these schemes (the best-known are *cursus planus, cursus tardus,* and *cursus velox*), fixed accentual patterns (*clausulae*) are used to produce rhythmic sentence-endings. Characteristically of the medieval attachment to the principle of hierarchy, the more complex and difficult of these were valued more highly than the simpler, and considered to achieve a more developed and admirable rhetorical or aesthetic effect. This principle underlies the gradations in Dante's critical judgements of the exemplary sentences in the remainder of II. vi. 4–5. 'Petrus amat multum dominam Bertam', however, ends in an accentual pattern that corresponds to none of the approved arrangements of *clausulae.* Also, its word-order is entirely straightforward and its vocabulary painfully ordinary. (The following examples show progressively greater degrees of complexity in these regards.) For all these reasons, though grammatically accurate as a sentence, it remains completely 'flavourless'.

123 Sharman (pp. 473–80) translates 'If it were not for my Above-All' (p. 477).

124 'So greatly does the thought of love please me'; see Stanislaw Stronski, *Le troubadour Folquet de Marseille: édition critique* (Cracow, 1910), pp. 15–18. Folquet (d. 1231) appears as a character in *Paradiso* IX, where his having

been a bishop seems to outweigh his having also – earlier in life – been a troubadour.

125 Wilhelm (pp. 62–5) translates 'I am the only one who knows the overwoe that rises' (p. 63).

126 'No man can accomplish fittingly'; see *Poésies du troubadour Aimeric de Belenoi*, edited by Maria Dumitrescu (Paris, 1935), pp. 84–9.

127 'Like the tree that, because it is weighed down'; see *The Poems of Aimeric de Péguilhan*, edited and translated by William P. Shepard and Frank M. Chambers (Evanston, 1950), pp. 233–6.

128 'Passion of love that dwells in my heart'; this poem is not by Thibaut de Champagne, as Dante clearly believed, but by his fellow *trouvère* Gace Brulé: see *The Lyrics and Melodies of Gace Brulé*, edited and translated by Samuel N. Rosenberg and Samuel Danon (New York, 1985).

129 See above, n. 50.

130 'I think it a foolish business, to tell the truth'; see Contini, II, pp. 450–2; Edwards, pp. 1–5 and 89–93.

131 'Since it is fitting that I bear a heart full of sorrow'; see Contini, II, p. 504. For an English version with commentary, see *The Poetry of Guido Cavalcanti*, edited and translated by Lowry Nelson, Jr (New York and London, 1986), pp. 18–19 and 93–4.

132 'Although I have for a long time'; see Marti, pp. 720–5.

133 'Love that speaks to me in my mind'; see Foster and Boyde, I, pp. 106–11 and II, pp. 173–83. The poem is subjected to prolonged exegesis in Book III of Dante's *Convivio*.

134 These canons of major Latin authors in, respectively, poetry and prose are remarkably interesting, in different ways. The poets are those whom one might expect, especially remembering the *Comedy* where Ovid and Lucan are part of the reception committee that greets Virgil and Dante in *Inferno* IV, Statius plays a major role in *Purgatorio* from canto XXI onwards, and Virgil is, of course, Dante's guide in both Hell and Purgatory. Only Horace – quoted, however, elsewhere in the *De vulgari eloquentia* itself (II. iv. 4) – seems to be missing from this list. There are, however, both some unexpected presences and some unexpected omissions in the list of prose writers. It is striking that Cicero, Augustine, and Boethius are not mentioned; and it is puzzling that Pliny and Frontinus – neither of whom is particularly distinguished for his style – are, especially since neither is present anywhere else in the substantial corpus of Dante's writings. Dante's 'affectionate interest' in Latin prose invites further consideration.

135 i.e., as a culture familiar with tobacco might have put it, 'pipe-dreams'.

136 'Mummy', 'Daddy', respectively in Tuscan and Central Italian (Umbrian?) forms.

137 'Sweetened', 'pleasant'; these forms are probably from Romagna, and their sound corresponds to Dante's pejorative description of that area's linguistic 'effeminacy' in I. xiv. 2, above.

138 'Flock', 'lyre'.

139 'Woman', 'body'.

140 It is worth noting that most of the words condemned here as inappropriate for serious lyric poetry are cheerfully used by Dante in the *Comedy*, where a different concept of genre and its conventions – not to mention of poetry in the vernacular – is clearly at work.

141 'Love', 'lady', 'desire', 'virtue', 'give', 'joy', 'health', 'safety', 'defence': all impeccably Tuscan, and also, perhaps not coincidentally, all key words in the thematics of Dante's own lyric poetry and that of his *stil novo* counterparts.

142 'Yes', 'no', 'me', 'you', 'him', 'at', 'and', 'the', 'or', 'where'.

143 'Land', 'honour', 'hope', 'weight', 'alleviated', 'impossibility', 'impossibility', 'most fortunately', 'most inanimately', 'most unfortunately', 'super-magnificently'.

144 This nonce-word, familiar to speakers of English from Shakespeare's *Love's Labour's Lost*, was a well-known novelty item in medieval dictionaries and grammar textbooks. Dante most probably found it in Uguccione da Pisa's *Magnae Derivationes*; see Paget Toynbee, 'Dante's Latin Dictionary', in *Dante Studies and Researches* (London, 1902; reprinted edition, 1971), pp. 97–114.

145 *Aeneid*, I. 1; 'I sing of arms and a man'.

146 'Ladies who have understanding of love'; see Foster and Boyde, I, pp. 59–63 and II, pp. 95–104. The poem appears in chapter XIX of Dante's *Vita nuova*.

147 The translation attempts to follow the Latin text's series of etymologically related terms, *gremium-ingremiat-congremiatio*. *Gremium* ('lap') is a common word in Latin; *ingremiare* is rare and non-classical (but occurs in Uguccione); *congremiatio* seems to be Dante's coinage. Likewise, 'lap' is normal English, 'enlap' is rare but in the *Oxford English Dictionary* and 'enlapment' is (I believe) a neologism, for which I am grateful to Peter Dronke.

148 Aristotle, *Physics*, I. 1. Dante would, of course, have read this in Latin translation, and probably with an accompanying commentary such as that of Thomas Aquinas. My translation of the periphrasis 'Magister Sapientum' is based – anachronistically, I admit – on *Inf.*, IV. 131.

149 'To the short day and the great circle of shadow'; see Foster and Boyde, I, pp. 162–5 and II, pp. 265–8.

150 This *canzone*, alas, has not survived, and the meaning of its isolated first line remains in dispute for lack of context. It seems to be something like 'Love draws the bar of my mind'; but how that image went on to be developed is anyone's guess. There is an interesting discussion of the subject by Barbara Spaggiari in *Dante Alighieri 1985: IN MEMORIAM HERMANN GMELIN*, edited by Richard Baum and Willi Hirdt (Tübingen, 1985), pp. 191–213.

151 See above, n. 121.
152 'A lady, tender in heart and young'; see Foster and Boyde, I, pp. 70–5 and
     II, pp. 114–20. The poem appears in chapter XXIII of the *Vita nuova*.
153 'Guido of Florence' is Cavalcanti: for this poem ('A lady begs me to
     discuss'), see Contini, II, pp. 522–9; Nelson, pp. 38–41 and 101–7.
154 See above, n. 146.
155 See above, n. 28.
156 See above, n. 126.
157 A truncated *canzone* beginning with this line has survived, but its identifi-
     cation with the poem cited by Dante is not universally accepted. For text
     and commentary, see Edwards, pp. 82–3 and 154.
158 This poem has not survived; see above, nn. 86 and 88.
159 Like its immediate predecessor in Dante's text, this poem is lost; see
     above, nn. 86 and 89.
160 See above, n. 153.
161 'Since Love has completely abandoned me'; see Foster and Boyde, I,
     pp. 138–47 and II, pp. 228–40. The editors suggest that this poem was
     'almost certainly destined for exposition in one of the unwritten treatises
     of the *Convivio*' (II, 228).
162 Marigo (p. 262) reads 'qua qualitate' ('what quality') for 'qualiter'.
163 Wilhelm (pp. 70–5) translates 'If Love were to me as broad in granting
     joy' (p. 71); Dante omits the words 'tant larga' at the line's end.
164 See above, n. 149.
165 Yet another – and perhaps the most – tantalising absence in the literary
     background of the *De vulgari eloquentia*: nothing whatever is known about
     the work of Gotto of Mantua, except that Dante admired it. This alone, of
     course, makes one want to know more.
166 i.e., Book II; for Dante's intention to discuss rhyme elsewhere in the *De
     vulgari eloquentia* – had it been finished – see II. xiii. 1.
167 'Love, you see well that this lady'; see Foster and Boyde, I, pp. 166–71 and
     II, pp. 268–72.
168 Literally, 'from right or left', in accordance with the common medieval alle-
     gorisation of those concepts that generates the figurative use of 'sinister'
     in modern English.

Index

Printed in the United States
89029LV00001B/205-237/A